MW00463258

REID SAUNDERS

WITH **SHANNON BUTCHER**
FOREWORD BY **GREG STIER**

Authors: Reid Saunders, Shannon Butcher

Printed in the United States of America.

Editing and proofing: Brett Butcher, Shannon Butcher, Karen Olson, Greg Stier

Cover/Interior Design: Kent Jensen | knail.com

TABLE OF CONTENTS

FOREWORD

GREG STIER

There are very few evangelists like Reid Saunders who are equally humble, hardworking, and hilarious. He not only passionately loves the Lord ("All for Jesus!") and people, but his burning passion to reach the lost with the Gospel is contagious.

One of the characteristics that sets him apart is that he genuinely understands the importance of training Christians to share their faith. In addition to doing large-scale evangelistic festivals across the world, Reid inspires and equips the Christians in every region he goes to for ongoing personal evangelism.

Reid understands that training believers to share the Gospel with their peers is the gift that keeps on giving. As the old saying goes, "Give a man a fish and he eats for a day. Teach a man to fish and he eats for a lifetime." Reid lives this out in powerful ways. He has trained churches around the world how to "fish for people."

This training focus ensures his evangelistic legacy will not be that of "blowing in, blowing up, and blowing out" of a city.

Instead, when Reid exits a region, he leaves behind a network of churches fully equipped to keep fishing for people long after his festival has gone.

For years, Reid and I have been partnering together in evangelism training. I count it an honor that he has used many Dare 2 Share resources to equip these churches to share their faith.

And now with *Active8*, Reid has his own powerful resource for equipping the saints to share the good news in a simple and clear way. My prayer is that you read this book, apply the practical ideas, and begin sharing your faith today!

And once you lead someone to Jesus, train that person to do the same, until everyone, everywhere hears, the greatest story ever told!

Let's Reach Them All!

Greg Stier
CEO & Founder, Dare 2 Share

ACKNOWLEDGMENTS

Carmen, I've never met anyone who loves Jesus and loves to tell others about Him more than you. This book is dedicated to you. I love you with all my heart and count it a true honor to be married to you for these past seventeen years. We have devoted our lives to sharing the Good News of Jesus to the ends of the earth. Carmen, your constant prayers, love, and support have made me the man I am today. I love you!

Azlan, Mylie, and Tobin, the three of you mean more to me than words can say. Every day, I praise Jesus that I am your dad and He has blessed me with each of you. I love each of you with all my heart and am so proud of you. I love serving Jesus with you, and I couldn't imagine my life without each of you playing such a special and important part. I look forward to more trips around the country and world sharing Jesus together.

Thank you RSA board and staff. We truly are a team and I couldn't do this without each of you. I love you all, and I want to thank you for serving Jesus with me! Thank you Brett Butcher, Phil Strom, Mike Bartlett, and Greg Stier for your input and feedback during the development of this book. Thank you Karen Olson for proofing the book. Thank you to John at

Church Art Works for the Active8 design and to Kent Jensen for doing another great job of cover design and typesetting!

Special thanks to my great friend, Shannon Butcher. You and Brett have served Jesus with me, practically from the beginning. I really appreciate you, Shannon, and all your hard work and sacrifice to make this book a reality. Thank you for helping me write this book and for all your support over the years.

Most of all, thank You Jesus, for giving me the joy of spending my life loving You and taking Your Good News to the ends of the earth. You are the One who has given me the desire to be active in sharing my faith. Please use Active8 to inspire countless brothers and sisters around the world to know You more and make You known! It's all for You!

All for Jesus,
Reid Saunders

MOTIVATION FOR SHARING YOUR FAITH

chapter 1

ACTIVE8

I loved growing up in Petaluma, California. I often think of the warm, summer breezes, the rolling hills of Napa Valley, and the breathtaking views of San Francisco Bay. Other memories that are dear to me are of friends from childhood and my adolescence.

There is one friend in particular I think of often – Jake. He and I were both wide receivers on the football team. Jake and I were inseparable during the weeks leading up to "daily doubles." If you have never played football, you might not know about this cruel and unusual punishment. During daily doubles, the team has two grueling practices every day in the heat of summer. The practices are to whip the team into shape after a long summer off.

Jake and I did our best to keep in shape all summer so we could survive the punishment! We would run routes, do drills, and sometimes finish the day with a long run. Afterward, we would catch our breaths underneath one of the huge eucalyptus trees that lined the park street. In between breaths, we would talk about everything – mostly football, girls, and more football.

I was not trying to hide my faith from Jake, I just never seemed to find the right moment to share Christ. I was a new Christian then, having come to faith in Christ at 17. I had grown up going to church only on holidays and special occasions. Even during those times at church, sharing your faith was never an emphasis. In fact, in some ways, evangelism was discouraged. Faith was a personal thing, I was told.

I realize now that I did not have any tools. Sure, I had the Scriptures, but carrying my heavy study Bible around wasn't really an option during receiver drills and five-mile runs. I needed something I could never lose, something I had memorized that would be easy, but not awkward, to share.

If you have read my book, *All for Jesus*, you may recall what happened next for Jake. One day, after we went for a run, he was in a car accident. Jake did not survive.

When I heard the news, I was in shock. We were invincible, or so it seemed. But now, my good buddy was dead and my heart was broken. Then it started to sink in... I never shared Jesus with Jake. I didn't know where Jake was now on the other side of eternity.

That moment was a turning point in my life. I realized that life is precious, it is short, and we never know how long we have on earth. I didn't want to miss another opportunity God gave me to share the Good News of Jesus with my friends.

In memory of Jake, and thinking of other friends and loved ones who are far from God, our team at Reid Saunders Association developed *Active8* to give you reasons and tools to share the Gospel.

Now, more than ever, we need to be equipped to share our faith. Did you know that in just the last seven years, the number of people in the United States who describe themselves as Christian has dropped eight percent? That means 25 million people who once identified themselves as Christian no longer do!

What are these former "Christians" turning to? Nothing, apparently. Rather, they now describe themselves as non-religious. Researchers call them the "Nones." What is even more shocking is that the younger the generation, the higher the percentage of "Nones."

Millennials (ages 18-30) have the highest percentage of non-religious people of any current generation. More than one third of all Millennials identify themselves as atheist, agnostic, or "nothing in particular." Something needs to change, and it needs to change quickly.

What can this change look like? Imagine an entire generation equipped to share their faith. Imagine this generation understanding and receiving the Gospel of Jesus Christ, then learning to share it. Imagine kids and adults alike knowing and memorizing the Good News and their testimony so they can readily explain to anyone who asks.

That's what *Active8* is all about. We released this book to help you share your faith by learning eight simple verses. You may know these verses; many in my generation learned them as the "Romans Road." These verses have been used for centuries to communicate the Good News with millions of people.

It is time for all of us to learn the biblical truths set forth in the "Romans Road." Through Active8, we are challenging the body of Christ to show their friends and family the way to eternal life through Jesus Christ. Our hope and prayer is that with Active8, we as believers will purposefully share our faith as a way of life, rather than seeing evangelism as a task or obligation.

WHAT IS ACTIVE8?

God wants to use your life to make a difference for eternity. The Apostle Paul writes in Philemon 1:6, "I pray that you may be active in sharing your faith, so that you will have a full understanding of every good thing we have in Christ."

The word "active" in Active8 comes from Paul's words in the above passage in Philemon. God calls us to be moving forward with the Good News. The 8 in Active8 comes from these eight verses in Romans

Romans 3:23; 5:1; 5:8; 6:23; 8:1; 10:9; 10:10; and 10:13.

I pray that you spend your life actively sharing your faith as you abide in God's love and give it away to others. With all my heart, I believe the greatest way you can show love to someone is to tell them about Jesus! May our Heavenly Father open doors for the Gospel wherever you go, and may you make the most of every opportunity He gives you to share your faith.

WHAT IS FAITH?

To break it down in the simplest of terms, faith is belief in something we cannot see with our eyes. As a Christian, faith is believing the Gospel, or Good News, presented in the Bible. So, what is the Good News? In his first letter to the church in Corinth, Paul spells it out plainly, (*NLT*, 1 Corinthians 15:1-9):

Let me now remind you, dear brothers and sisters, of the Good News I preached to you before. You welcomed it then, and you still stand firm in it. It is this Good News that saves you if you continue to believe the message I told you—unless, of course, you believed something that was never true in the first place.

I passed on to you what was most important and what had also been passed on to me. Christ died for our sins, just as the Scriptures said. He was buried, and he was raised from the dead on the third day, just as the Scriptures said. He was seen by Peter and then by the Twelve. After that, he was seen by more than 500 of his followers at one time, most of whom are still alive, though some have died. Then he was seen by James and later by all the apostles. Last of all, as though I had been born at the wrong time, I also saw him. For I am the least of all the apostles. In fact,

I'm not even worthy to be called an apostle after the way I persecuted God's church.

These two paragraphs from Paul tell us a great deal. So, let's unpack them a bit. First, Paul introduces the Good News by reminding the Corinthians that he preached it to them in the past. Then he points out that by believing in that Good News, they are saved.

So here it is, the Good News:

1. Christ died for our sins.
2. He was buried and raised from the dead on the third day.

That's it! Isn't it simple?

After stating the Good News, Paul emphasizes that there were witnesses to Christ's death and resurrection. First Peter and the twelve saw Jesus, then more than 500 of his followers, James and all the apostles, and lastly Paul.

Aren't you glad that our faith does not have to be blind or unreasonable? Jesus provided us with a critical piece of evidence for His miraculous resurrection – more than 500 eyewitnesses!

So what if the Good News is a verified miraculous event that occurred more than 2000 years ago? What difference does that make for you and me?

This is where things get personal.

We go beyond observing a historic event, and we examine our own hearts. Inside of you and me is a deadly plague that destroys us – sin. We were born with it and we chose it ourselves, time and time again, beginning in our childhood and continuing to this day. The cost of sin is great. If you and I were to pay the price for our sin, it would be our very lives, and would be separated from God for eternity.

We'll go into Scripture references a little later, but for now, let's stay focused on why the Good News matters to you and me personally.

Please take a few minutes to reflect or journal about where you might be if you had not heard and believed the Good News of Jesus. What might it be like to walk through life bearing the burden of your sin and shame?

Now, take another few minutes to talk to Jesus and thank Him. He paid the cost of all your wrongdoing, He suffered at the hands of people who hated and beat him. He willingly laid down His life, receiving nails in His hands and feet and agonizing on a rugged, wooden cross... for you. Because He loves you. Because He didn't want to live in heaven without you.

I hope you are able to let that sink into your heart, mind, and spirit – every part of you. Breathe it in.

JESUS LOVES YOU

He paid the price you could never pay so your Heavenly Father could adopt you as His own child. He loves you more than you can imagine.

Receive that truth in faith and continue to walk in it for the rest of your life. Everything else in this book is secondary. Your own faith in Jesus must come first before you can effectively share it with anyone else. It seems like a no-brainer, but if we're honest, we've all been guilty of neglecting our own faith and relationship with Jesus.

I wonder if you will make a decision right now to nurture, instead of neglect, your faith.

If you have ever planted anything, you know that a plant needs good soil, water, and light in order to flourish. In a similar way, our faith is like a plant (or a mustard seed). Our faith needs God's Word, communication with God Himself through prayer and worship, and relationship with others who love Him.

Our faith is also like a muscle. If we exercise or lift weights, our muscles get stronger and larger. If we are inactive, our muscles atrophy. Likewise, our faith grows and is strengthened when we serve Him in our world and when we share Him with those who don't yet know and/or believe the Good News.

ACTIVE8

There are many Bible verses which explain the hope of the Gospel. Active8 is the following eight verses, also known as the Romans Road.

Romans 3:23 –
"For all have sinned and fall short of the glory of God."

Romans 5:1 –
"Therefore, since we have been justified through faith, we have peace with God through our Lord Jesus Christ…."

Romans 5:8 –
"But God demonstrates His own love for us in this: While we were still sinners, Christ died for us."

Romans 6:23 –
"For the wages of sin is death, but the gift of God is eternal life through Christ Jesus our Lord."

Romans 8:1 –
"Therefore, there is now no condemnation for those who are in Christ Jesus."

Romans 10:9 –
"…If you confess with your mouth, 'Jesus is Lord,' and believe in your heart that God raised him from the dead, you will be saved."

Romans 10:10 –
"For it is with your heart that you believe and are justified, and it is with your mouth that you confess and are saved."

Romans 10:13 –
"Everyone who calls on the name of the Lord will be saved."

It would help you tremendously to do three things with Active8:

1. Open your Bible and read each of these verses in context; in fact, reading the entire book of Romans is a great idea. If you like, highlight Active8 in your Bible.
2. Write each of the Active8 verses on a note card or something so you can refer to them again and again.

3. Commit each verse of Active8 to memory. As you memorize, remember what the verse means in context of the book of Romans and especially the verses that come before and after the one you are memorizing. Carry your Active8 note cards in your purse or pocket and look at them throughout the day. By doing this you can usually memorize a verse in a week or so.

I'll close each chapter with a prayer; the first one is my prayer for you:

Father in heaven, please bless my brothers and sisters reading this. Please help them to read, understand, and memorize Active8. Bless them with mustard seed faith, and help them to nurture that faith so it grows tall and strong.

Please help them to live in relationship with You constantly, reading Your Word every day and allowing You to speak to them through it. Help them to seek out opportunities to serve You where they live and around the world. May you pour your Holy Spirit on them and help their faith to shine light in the darkness. May they walk in the truth that You love them deeply, that you like them too, and that You have good plans for their lives.

May they put on the full armor of God each day and stand firm, holding up their shield of faith to guard them from the enemy's flaming arrows. May they wield the sword of the Spirit by knowing, memorizing, and meditating on your Holy Word. May Your Word renew their minds and change them from the inside out to become more like your Son, our Savior Jesus. In Jesus' Name, Amen.

WHO IS JESUS?

The identity of Jesus is a critical part of sharing the Gospel, because many people say they know about Jesus or they might even say that they worship Him. Who is Jesus, though? There are many different ideas about who He is, so you need to make sure you present Jesus clearly from the Scriptures.

Many people have not read the Bible for themselves or listened to clear instruction from it. They may have heard about Jesus from false teachers, who take some truth about Jesus and distort it, leave parts out, or add to it. I have even traveled to places in the world where people have never even heard the name of Jesus.

Jesus was not simply a teacher, a miracle-worker, a prophet, a son of God, or a good man. He also was not a crazy person or a deceiver. He was, and is, the only begotten Son of God, God incarnate, who left His place of honor in heaven to dwell among us on earth. On earth, He redeemed us from sin by laying down His life as a substitute for us, paying the full price of our sin. Then, He returned to heaven, where He is seated now and intercedes for us on a daily basis.

There are entire books written about the person of Jesus Christ. We will simply look at some bullet points with Scripture references to give an overview. These are some of the most important things to know about Jesus as we prepare to share Him with others. Please take the time to look up each reference. It would be a good idea to memorize some of the following verses as well.

- Jesus is God. He is eternal and was present with the Father during Creation (John 1:1-3; Revelation 1:17-18).
- Jesus *is the Son of Man and Son of God (John 3:13-18).*
- Jesus is the Messiah and the Lamb of God and He is worthy of worship (John 1:29-34; Revelation 5:8-14).
- Jesus was born of a virgin, Mary (Matthew 1:18).
- Jesus was born in a real, human body (1 John 1:4-6).
- Jesus performed many miracles (Matthew 11:20).
- Jesus fulfilled prophecies of the Messiah (John 12:14-16).
- Jesus was condemned and crucified because He claimed to be God. The Jewish leaders did not believe Him, so they accused Jesus of blasphemy (Matthew 26:57-68; John 5:16-18; 8:57-59).
- Jesus lived a sinless life. He was innocent (2 Corinthians 5:21; Matthew 27:1-6; Matthew 27:19).
- Jesus physically died (John 19:31-37).
- Jesus died in our place, paying our death penalty (Romans 3:23-26; 5:8).
- Jesus' blood cleanses us from all sin (1 John 1:7-10).
- Jesus rose from the grave (Matthew 28:1-10).
- Jesus gave the Holy Spirit to His disciples (John 20:19-23).
- Jesus commissioned His followers to preach the Good News and make disciples (Matthew 28:16-20).
- Jesus ascended into heaven (Acts 1:6-11).
- Jesus is coming back (Matthew 26:64; Revelation 1:7).
- Jesus is King of kings, and Lord of lords (Philippians 2:5-11; Revelation 19:11-16).
- The Father has given Jesus authority to judge (John 5:25-30).
- Jesus loves us (John 15:9; Revelation 1:4-6).

I encourage you to pray in response to these verses.

Father, God, thank You for Jesus. Thank You for revealing so much about Him through Your Scriptures. Thank You for counting my life at such a high value that You sent Jesus to earth to receive the judgment I deserved.

Father, You raised Jesus from the grave and gave Him all authority to rule and judge. I honor Jesus as King of kings, and Lord of lords who was, and is, and is to come. I long for His glorious return.

Please help me to get to know Jesus better, hiding Your Word about Him in my heart, and sharing Him with others out of my deep love for Him. In Jesus' Name, Amen.

WHY WE SHARE OUR FAITH

After Jesus rose from the dead and before He ascended into heaven, He entrusted His followers with a weighty charge, referred to by many as the Great Commission (*NLT*, Matthew 28:16-20):

Jesus came and told his disciples, "I have been given all authority in heaven and on earth. Therefore, go and make disciples of all the nations, baptizing them in the name of the Father and the Son and the Holy Spirit. Teach these new disciples to obey all the commands I have given you. And be sure of this: I am with you always, even to the end of the age."

Simply stated, one reason we share our faith is because Jesus told us to make disciples. As we make disciples, we baptize people and teach them the Word of God. Sharing the Good News of Jesus is an integral part of making disciples.

It is important for us to obey, but my hope and prayer for you is that you witness to others because you are motivated by love rather than by obligation. Obedience that comes from love is far different than obedience driven by fear of punishment.

As John talks about love, he explains in 1 John 4:18, "Such love has no fear, because perfect love expels all fear. If we are afraid, it is for fear of punishment, and this shows that we have not fully experienced his perfect love."

When we experience God's perfect love, it changes us so that we no longer operate in fear. Think of it, would you rather have someone share their life with you out of fear or out of love?

We want to offer others the gift of eternal life through Christ out of our deep love for God and for them. Trust me, people will be much more open to hearing about Jesus if they believe that you are sharing out of love.

LOVE AND OBEDIENCE

It's interesting to note that in the Bible, love and obedience are linked. Jesus told His disciples in John 14:15 (*NLT*), "If you love me, obey my commandments." And later in the same chapter in verse 21, Jesus explains: "Those who accept my commandments and obey them are the ones who love me. And because they love me, my Father will love them. And I will love them and reveal myself to each of them."

Obedience is a healthy response to loving someone, particularly a mother, father, guardian, or God.

In John 15:10 (*NLT*), in the context of Jesus telling us to remain in the vine, He says "When you obey my commandments, you remain in my love, just as I obey my Father's commandments and remain in his love."

As He does so many times, Jesus not only teaches us a truth, He lives it out. He modeled obedience to the Father out of love and calls us to obey Him out of love in the same way.

We can even go all the way back to the Ten Commandments to find that the Lord promises to "lavish unfailing love for a thousand generations on those who love me and obey my commands" (Exodus 20:6). Many more times in the Scriptures we find this coupling of love and obedience.

Therefore, when Jesus tells us to make disciples, we have the opportunity to show that we love Him by obeying His commandment. It may seem scary or intimidating, but we have Jesus' own words to encourage us as we step out in obedience and faith: "And be sure of this: I am with you always, even to the end of the age" (*NLT*, Matthew 28:20b). Doesn't it encourage you to know that when you make disciples, you're not doing it alone? Jesus has promised to always be with you. And He will give you the open doors, the courage, and the words to say.

SUFFERING FOR THE GOSPEL

Sometimes, we might share the Gospel out of fear that God will punish us if we do not obey. On the flipside, we may be silent in fear that people will reject us. Some may fear losing a close relationship, a job, or even their own life. In my travels, I have met some of these dear brothers and sisters who have lost much for the sake of following Christ.

Jesus was no stranger to persecution. He prophesied His betrayal and crucifixion. In Mark 8:31 (*NLT*), Jesus told his disciples "that the Son of Man must suffer many terrible things and be rejected by the elders, the leading priests, and the teachers of religious law. He would be killed, but three days later he would rise from the dead."

Jesus clearly understood that His message would cost Him a great deal. But there was something more important to Jesus than impending betrayal, rejection, suffering, and death – joy.

Hebrews 12:2 instructs us, "Let us fix our eyes on Jesus, the author and perfecter of our faith, who for the joy set before him endured the cross, scorning its shame, and sat down at the right hand of the throne of God."

What was the joy that was before Jesus? I believe that joy was thinking of you. Jesus could see into the future and thought of the day that you would believe in Him. He was thinking of that moment, and as you received Him He exchanged your death sentence for the gift of eternal life.

He was thinking of me, and each one in the body of Christ. He was thinking of those yet to hear and receive the Good News.

It's hard to imagine a person having the kind of love and longsuffering that tolerates rejection again and again, yet still reaches out for relationship. Yet, that is exactly the love that Jesus and the Father in Heaven have for you and me, and every person in the world.

GOD'S PATIENCE AND LONGING

We read in 2 Peter 3:9 (*NLT*), "The Lord isn't really being slow about his promise, as some people think. No, he is being patient for your sake. He does not want anyone to be destroyed, but wants everyone to repent."

I'll admit, sometimes I grow impatient and want Jesus to come back RIGHT NOW! There are days when I want Him to right every wrong and judge those who are bent on evil. Yet, when I look at 2 Peter 3:9, I realize that our Father in Heaven has a very different perspective. He is waiting to judge so that more people will turn to Him and be saved. Our Lord is not looking forward to wiping people out. Instead, He longs to redeem them!

Jesus helped us understand the Father's longing as He taught the parables of the lost sheep, the lost coin, and the lost son in Luke 15. If you have a Bible, I recommend reading the whole chapter right now. Here is a section of it that tells about the lost sheep (*NLT*, Luke 15:3-7):

So Jesus told them this story: "If a man has a hundred sheep and one of them gets lost, what will he do? Won't he leave the ninety-nine others in the wilderness and go to search for the one that is lost until he finds it? And when he has found it, he will joyfully carry it home on his shoulders. When he arrives, he will call together his friends and neighbors, saying, 'Rejoice with me because I have found my lost sheep.' In the same way, there is more joy in heaven over one lost sinner who repents and returns to God than over ninety-nine others who are righteous and haven't strayed away!

We learn from His Word that the Father is deeply concerned about the lost – those who have wandered away from Him and those who have never known Him. He searches and seeks out the one who is far from Him. God searched for you, and He searched for me. He is searching for people you know who are far from Him. When you wander from Him, God searches for you again, brings you back, and welcomes you home.

GOD REALLY, REALLY LOVES YOU!!!

If you have the recording or access to it on the internet, take a moment to listen to Stuart Townend's "How Deep the Father's Love for Us" and/or Chris Tomlin's "Jesus Loves Me." If it helps, close your eyes, sing along or just listen, whatever helps you receive the truth of those songs best.

There are many songs that express the profound love that God has for us. It is good for us to sing them often, to memorize Scriptures about God's love for us, and to meditate on the truth that God loves us – deeply, unconditionally, and eternally.

Remember why Jesus chose people to follow Him, why He preached the Gospel, why He served and performed miracles. Make it personal – remember why Jesus endured the cross to save you from your death sentence and give you abundant and eternal life.

He loves you!

And it brought Him joy in His hour of torment to think of you belonging to Him... forever.

As you live in that grace, that love, and that sacrifice, it softens you, changes you, helps you to see yourself and others in a way that aligns more closely with God's heart.

People often ask me how they can be more effective in sharing Jesus with others. I have found that the key to being mission-minded and bringing our friends to Jesus is to fall so deeply in love with Jesus that telling others about Him comes naturally. To illustrate, let me tell you a story about a little boy and his pastor.

One day after church a boy came up to his pastor in the parking lot and said, "Pastor, during your sermon you said I could ask Jesus into my heart to be my Savior."

"That's right," the pastor replied. The little boy scratched his head and looked confused.

He said, "But Pastor, Jesus was a man in a man's body right?"

"Yes, that is true" the Pastor replied.

The boy continued, "So, if Jesus was a man in a man's body and I'm just a little boy in a little boy's body, if I ask Jesus into my heart, He will be sticking out all over!"

The Pastor replied, "Exactly!"

The closer you and I are in our relationship with Jesus, the more He will be "sticking out" all over in our lives. I have found that the greatest joy in life is knowing Jesus and making Him known. This comes from spending time with Jesus in prayer and the Word.

Acts 4:13 records what the religious leaders said after being around Peter and John. "When they saw the courage of Peter and John and realized that they were unschooled, ordinary men, they took note that these men had been with Jesus." Spending time with Jesus makes all the difference, and it certainly comes naturally to spend time with the one we love.

When my wife Carmen and I were dating, I couldn't wait to be with her. I wanted to know everything about her. Nobody had to tell me to spend time with Carmen, I was motivated by love.

Even after years of marriage, I still look forward to seeing Carmen when I come home from work. When I travel for days, I miss her, and I can't wait to see her again when I come home!

When we love Jesus, we can't wait to be with Him either. We cherish times of corporate and private worship. We long for uninterrupted, quiet time to talk with Him and hear from His Word. We come to meet with Him out of love instead of obligation.

WHAT IS LOVE?

In 1 Corinthians 13:4-8, we find one of the most thorough descriptions of love in the Scriptures:

> *Love is patient and kind. Love is not jealous or boastful or proud or rude. It does not demand its own way. It is not irritable, and it keeps no record of being wronged. It does not rejoice about injustice but rejoices whenever the truth wins out. Love never gives up, never loses faith, is always hopeful, and endures through every circumstance.*

God gave us an explanation of love with words, but He also demonstrated it throughout history, with the ultimate example of Christ giving His own life for us. As the passage on love closes, God gives an important comparison (*NLT*, 1 Corinthians 13:13): "Three things will last forever – faith, hope, and love – and the greatest of these is love."

It's interesting to me to see God compare these three things. To say that faith is important is an understatement. Truly, without faith we cannot possibly please God (Hebrews 11:6), and we can't be saved without faith (Romans 10:9-10).

Yet, in comparison with faith, LOVE is even more important. Love is greater than faith. Love is the greatest thing that will last forever.

That truth is a game-changer, in every aspect of our lives. If God considers love to be greater than faith, and He certainly wants us to have faith, then how much more does He desire for us to live in love?

In Ephesians 3:14-19 (*NLT*), the Apostle Paul delivers a powerful prayer for those who follow Jesus Christ:

When I think of all this, I fall to my knees and pray to the Father, the Creator of everything in heaven and on earth. I pray that from his glorious, unlimited resources he will empower you with inner strength through his Spirit. Then Christ will make his home in your hearts as you trust in him. Your roots will grow down into God's love and keep you strong. And may you have the power to understand, as all God's people should, how wide, how long, how high, and how deep his love is. May you experience the love of Christ, though it is too great to understand fully. Then you will be made complete with all the fullness of life and power that comes from God.

Wow! What a blessing! What a request! I want that, for me and for you! I want Jesus making His home in us. I want our roots to grow deep into God's love, and for us to grasp that love that's beyond understanding. I want us to be made complete. Don't you want all that, too?

If you are like me and you want your life to make a difference for eternity, if you want to share your faith with others and watch Jesus change lives like I do, then our roots must grow deep in the love of God.

As Paul begins the love chapter we just looked at, he points out, "...if I had such faith that I could move mountains, but didn't love others, I would be nothing" (*NLT*, 1 Corinthians 13:2b). Is faith important? It's paramount! But if it's not paired with love, it's worthless! This is a message we cannot afford to miss!

I do not want to stand before my Father in Heaven one day and see that all the work of sharing my faith was in vain. I want to be rooted in God's love as I live my everyday life with my wife and three kids, every time I step into a meeting, and every time I step onto a stage and grab a microphone. If I'm not walking in love, my life isn't worth much.

Please pray this prayer from your heart to God:

Father, You are Creator of everything in heaven and on earth. You have taught me about Your love from the beginning of Genesis to the end of Revelation. You have shown me Your love throughout history, and in my own life. You loved the world so much that You gave Your only begotten Son, Jesus. I believe that You love me and allowed Jesus to die in my place. I receive Your love.

Please search my heart. Have I acted in faith without love?

I want to be found faithful AND loving. Please help me to walk in Your love and in faith. In Jesus' Name, Amen.

THE URGENCY OF THE GOSPEL

Billy Graham once said, "The evangelistic harvest is always urgent. The destiny of men, women, and of nations is always being decided. Every generation is strategic. We are not responsible for the past generation, and we cannot bear the full responsibility for the next one, but we do have our generation. God will hold us responsible as to how well we fulfill our responsibilities to this age and take advantage of our opportunities."

The Apostle Paul urges in 2 Corinthians 6:1-2, "As God's partners, we beg you not to accept this marvelous gift of God's kindness and then ignore it. For God says, 'At just the right time, I heard you. On the day of salvation, I helped you.' Indeed, the 'right time' is now. Today is the day of salvation."

Every day, people all over the world die, destined to face judgment before God's throne. They cannot afford for us to delay. Today is the day of salvation. Not tomorrow. Not next week. Today.

Part of the Romans Road tells us that, "...everyone has sinned; we all fall short of God's glorious standard," (*NLT*, Romans

3:23) and "...the wages of sin is death, but the free gift of God is eternal life through Christ Jesus our Lord," (*NLT*, Romans 6:23). You, every other human being, and I are born into the same condition. We are sinners deserving of death. And unless Jesus returns first, every one of us will die.

Jesus is clear in the Gospels that those who do not know Him will suffer in a place of torment we call Hell. Jesus refers to it as "outer darkness, where there will be weeping and gnashing of teeth," (*NLT*, Matthew 25:30). In that same chapter of Matthew, Jesus reveals a scene of judgment to come in the future (*NLT*, Matthew 25:31-46).

> *"But when the Son of Man comes in his glory, and all the angels with him, then he will sit upon his glorious throne. All the nations will be gathered in his presence, and he will separate the people as a shepherd separates the sheep from the goats. He will place the sheep at his right hand and the goats at his left.*

> *"Then the King will say to those on his right, 'Come, you who are blessed by my Father, inherit the Kingdom prepared for you from the creation of the world. For I was hungry, and you fed me. I was thirsty, and you gave me a drink. I was a stranger, and you invited me into your home. I was naked, and you gave me clothing. I was sick, and you cared for me. I was in prison, and you visited me.'*

> *"Then these righteous ones will reply, 'Lord, when did we ever see you hungry and feed you? Or thirsty and give you something to drink? Or a stranger and show you hospitality? Or naked and give you clothing? When did we ever see you sick or in prison and visit you?'*

> *"And the King will say, 'I tell you the truth, when you did it to one of the least of these my brothers and sisters, you were doing it to me!'*

> *"Then the King will turn to those on the left and say, 'Away with you, you cursed ones, into the eternal fire prepared*

for the devil and his demons. For I was hungry, and you didn't feed me. I was thirsty, and you didn't give me a drink. I was a stranger, and you didn't invite me into your home. I was naked, and you didn't give me clothing. I was sick and in prison, and you didn't visit me.'

"Then they will reply, 'Lord, when did we ever see you hungry or thirsty or a stranger or naked or sick or in prison, and not help you?'

"And he will answer, 'I tell you the truth, when you refused to help the least of these my brothers and sisters, you were refusing to help me.'

"And they will go away into eternal punishment, but the righteous will go into eternal life."

Just as this passage in Matthew makes me uncomfortable, I'm guessing it does the same to you. I don't like thinking of God as one who punishes people in eternal fire. Yet, there it is, in Scripture. We can try to avoid it, but the fact is, it's there. It's true. And a time is coming when all of us will be held accountable for what we believe and what we do (or don't do).

It's a hard passage too, because all of us know people who don't yet follow Christ. And if they were to die today and face judgment, they would be cast into eternal fire rather than inheriting eternal life. I don't wish that on my worst enemies, but to think of some of the people I dearly love suffering that fate is TERRIFYING.

Therefore, I (and likely you, as well) have a sense of urgency. We must share the Good News with people so that they can know and receive Jesus Christ and His gift of eternal life.

In Luke 12:4, Jesus teaches, "Dear friends, don't be afraid of those who want to kill your body; they cannot do any more to you after that. But I'll tell you whom to fear. Fear God, who has the power to kill you and then throw you into hell. Yes, he's the one to fear." We learn from Jesus that God the Father has the authority to throw people into hell. And we should fear Him for that.

It seems like a strange idea to fear God. After all, isn't He loving and kind and good? Why would we fear someone with those characteristics? We should fear Him simply because God tells us to fear Him. In Deuteronomy 6:24 we read, "And the LORD our God commanded us to obey all these decrees and to fear him so he can continue to bless us and preserve our lives, as he has done to this day. Throughout the book of Proverbs, we are told that the fear of the Lord is the beginning of wisdom (Proverbs 9:10). Fear of the Lord is an important thread woven through the tapestry of Scripture.

So we understand that there is a significant, life-changing cost to our decision to share our faith or to keep it to ourselves. Perhaps it will help clarify our choice if we realize that we must choose whom we fear – do we fear God or do we fear people? Do we fear the eternal consequences of a loving Judge or do we fear the finite losses we may face on earth?

The choice is yours.

JOHN HARPER

When I think about having a passion and urgency to share the Good News of Jesus, I'm reminded of the story of John Harper. This story is contained in *The Mission of an Evangelist* (Billy Graham Association 285-286):

> It was April 15, 1912, when the HMS Titanic sank beneath the icy waters of the North Atlantic, taking with it 1,517 lives. The largest and most luxurious ship at the time was gone, reminding the world of our frailty as human beings. But there is more to the sinking of the Titanic than a historical tragedy. There is a story of courageous heroism and unshakable faith.

> John Harper was aboard the Titanic when she set sail from Southampton, England, on her maiden voyage. An evangelist originally from Glasgow, Scotland, he was well known throughout the United Kingdom as a charismatic,

passionate speaker who led many to Christ through his preaching. In 1912, Reverend Harper received an invitation to speak at the Moody Church in Chicago, U.S.A. On April 11, 1912, John Harper boarded the Titanic.

Some of the wealthiest people in the world were aboard. While many passengers spoke of business deals, acquisitions, and material desires, John Harper was diligently sharing the love of Christ with others. In the days leading up to the tragedy, survivors reported seeing Harper living like a man of faith, speaking kind words and sharing the love of Christ.

On the evening of April 14, as passengers danced in the ballroom and tried their luck at the card tables, John Harper put his daughter to bed and read his devotions as he did every night. At 11:40 p.m., the Titanic struck an iceberg. The "unsinkable" ship was doomed. Either in disbelief or unaware at the time, passengers continued about their pleasures. It wasn't until the ship's crew sent up a series of distress flares that passengers realized the seriousness of their situation. Then chaos ensued.

It all happened so fast. But John Harper's response left an historic example of courage and faith. Harper awakened his daughter, picked her up and wrapped her in a blanket before carrying her up to the deck. There he kissed her good-bye and handed her to a crewman who put her into lifeboat number 11. Harper knew he would never see his daughter again. His daughter would be left an orphan at six years of age. Harper then gave his life jacket to a fellow passenger, ending any chance of his own survival. From a survivor we learn that he was calling out, 'Women and children and unsaved people into the lifeboats." So he understood that there was a more important thing than surviving that terrible disaster. He understood that there were those who were unprepared to face eternity.

As the sounds of terror and mayhem continued, Harper focused on his God-given purpose. Survivors reported seeing him on the upper deck on his knees, surrounded by terrified passengers, praying for their salvation.

At 2:40 a.m., the Titanic disappeared beneath the North Atlantic, leaving a mushroom-like cloud of smoke and steam above her grave and, tragically, over 1,000 people, including Harper, fighting for their lives in the icy water. He managed to find a piece of floating wreckage to hold onto. Quickly he swam to every person he could find, urging those about him to put their faith in Jesus Christ. While death forced others to face the folly of their life's pursuits, John Harper's goal of winning people to Jesus Christ became more vital.

In the water, John Harper was moving around as best he could, speaking to as many people as possible. His question was, "Are you saved?" And if they weren't saved and if they didn't understand that terminology, then as rapidly as he could he explained the Christian Gospel.

Soon John Harper succumbed to the icy sea. But even in his last moment, this tireless man of undying faith continued his life pursuit of winning lost souls.

One person remembered, "I am a survivor of the Titanic. I was one of only six people out of 1,517 to be pulled from the icy waters on that dreadful night. Like the hundreds around me, I found myself struggling in the cold, dark waters of the North Atlantic. The wail of the perishing was ringing in my ears when there floated by me a man who called to me, 'Is your soul saved?' Then I heard him call out to others as he and everyone around me sank beneath the waters. There, alone in the night with two miles of water under me, I cried out to Christ to save me. I am John Harper's last convert."

Powerful! We must be ready at all times and make the most of every opportunity God gives us. My prayer is that you become more passionate about actively sharing Jesus with your friends, family, and anyone else God leads you to disciple.

God may or may not place us in a historic tragedy like He did with John Harper. But we can be confident that the everyday opportunities of interacting with people in our world are just as important, and perhaps even the testing and training ground for more dramatic opportunities.

John Harper proved faithful in the mundane, in the routine, and in continually sowing into His relationship with God. It may be that God entrusted John to be on board the Titanic, knowing that many would trust in Christ through his witness, because John was faithful in the "small stuff."

Let's pray:

Jesus, you lived on this earth with great purpose. Your every word and action was intentional. You always had eternity in mind, and it allowed you to endure suffering beyond what we've ever experienced.

Please help us to walk with You, to examine the way You lived on earth as we examine our own life. Holy Spirit, please convict us of apathy, of ways we've grown too comfortable in our life here on earth. Show us when we have forsaken our eternal identity for our temporal one. Please help us to live like you and like John Harper and others who understand their purpose on earth.

We ask for Your protection from the enemy, with his serpent's ways, trying to distract us and draw us away from our real life in you. Help us to not accept counterfeit life and purpose for your destiny for us. In Jesus' Name.

SHOW AND TELL

When I was in kindergarten, I always looked forward to "show and tell." And now, more than thirty years later, I've witnessed each of my three children go through that phase of life, as well. There is something precious about watching the face of a young child light up as they share something special with their classmates. I love hearing their excited little voices as they tell other kids why their show and tell item means so much to them.

Do you remember a time in your life where you were that excited to tell others about something? Maybe it was an award that you won, a picture that you can't wait to show to a friend, or getting hired for your first job.

Have you ever been that excited to share with others what God is doing in your life? When we tell others about Jesus, I pray that God gives us the same enthusiasm as a kindergarten student showing their favorite toy!

Many times in Scripture, when people believed in Jesus, their response was to bring their family members and friends to meet Jesus. It came naturally to them to tell others about what they had seen.

One example is found in John 1:41-42, "The first thing Andrew did was to find his brother Simon and tell him, 'We have found the Messiah' (that is, the Christ). And he brought him to Jesus."

If you have spent much time in the New Testament, you'll realize that the Simon referred to in this verse is the man who Jesus later calls "Peter." Peter becomes one of the most important people in the foundation of Christianity and the church. And his faith in Christ began because his brother couldn't help but share Jesus with him.

I've had the privilege of seeing many modern-day Andrews bring their Simons to Jesus. Our team at RSA works with local churches in the United States and around the world to train them in friendship evangelism.

We encourage the pastors and local church members in many of the same ways I'm encouraging you in this book. We teach them about Jesus' commandment to make disciples and share practical ways to pray, share, and invite others to their evangelistic event. Then our team comes to help the churches hold an evangelistic festival.

In September, 2015, our team held a festival in Córdoba, Argentina, where we saw God move in a mighty way. More than 35,000 people came to the festival and over 7,500 people gave their lives to Jesus! To God be the glory!

It was amazing to see the churches come together to reach the youth for Jesus! Córdoba is an extremely unreached place, and there are thousands of youth in this city who have no hope.

As a result, the young believers in Córdoba wanted to reach their friends for Jesus. They showed them about Jesus as they loved on their friends and invited them to hear about Jesus at the festival.

One of my favorite things to see is people raise their hands or come toward the front of the stage to indicate their decision to receive Jesus. But what I love almost as much is seeing those people coming forward with their friends who are rejoicing that they came to Jesus! God did that in Córdoba, as He has in so many other places in the world.

CAN'T KEEP QUIET

When I think about the idea of "showing and telling" our friends about Jesus I'm reminded of a story in 2 Kings. The king of Aram had besieged Samaria, and the people there were starving.

Then Elisha prophesied that God was about to bountifully provide for them. The part if this story that I want to share is about four lepers (*NLT*, 2 Kings 7:3-11):

Now there were four men with leprosy sitting at the entrance of the city gates. "Why should we sit here waiting to die?" they asked each other. "We will starve if we stay here, but with the famine in the city, we will starve if we go back there. So we might as well go out and surrender to the Aramean army. If they let us live, so much the better. But if they kill us, we would have died anyway."

So at twilight they set out for the camp of the Arameans. But when they came to the edge of the camp, no one was there! For the Lord had caused the Aramean army to hear the clatter of speeding chariots and the galloping of horses and the sounds of a great army approaching. "The king of Israel has hired the Hittites and Egyptians to attack us!" they cried to one another. So they panicked and ran into the night, abandoning their tents, horses, donkeys, and everything else, as they fled for their lives.

When the men with leprosy arrived at the edge of the camp, they went into one tent after another, eating and drinking wine; and they carried off silver and gold and clothing and hid it. Finally, they said to each other, "This is not right. This is a day of good news, and we aren't sharing it with anyone! If we wait until morning, some calamity will certainly fall upon us. Come on, let's go back and tell the people at the palace."

So they went back to the city and told the gatekeepers what had happened. "We went out to the Aramean camp," they said, "and no one was there! The horses and donkeys were tethered and the tents were all in order, but there wasn't a single person around!" Then the gatekeepers shouted the news to the people in the palace.

Once news got to the king, he had some of his officers make sure the Arameans hadn't set a trap. Once they discovered the Arameans had fled the area completely, all the people went out and plundered the Arameans. Then Elisha's prophecy was fulfilled. God had provided bountifully, and the people were saved from their enemies.

It's interesting how the lepers went from selfishly enjoying the plunder to thinking about the bigger picture. Let's look at verse 9 again: "Finally, they said to each other, 'This is not right. This is a day of good news, and we aren't sharing it with anyone! If we wait until morning, some calamity will certainly fall upon us. Come on, let's go back and tell the people at the palace.'"

The lepers realized two things: 1) that the good news wasn't just for them, it was meant to be shared; and 2) there would be judgment if they kept this good news to themselves.

In the same way, God has allowed you and me to discover the Good News of Jesus. We have enjoyed the benefits of salvation – forgiveness of sin, a clear conscience, friendship with God, the fruit of the Spirit, and the list could go on and on. Maybe we even have a close group of friends at church with whom we have enjoyed these blessings.

But perhaps God is using this book to help you see the bigger picture. There is a whole world out there who doesn't know the Good News yet. There are people in your city, your neighborhood, your church, maybe even your own household, who don't know it. They are starving in spiritual famine while we enjoy the lavish blessings of being adopted by the King of Kings and Lord of Lords.

Jesus was never meant to be a secret. He doesn't want us to keep the Good News to ourselves. Rather, He wants us to share Him with our "city" – literally and figuratively. We need to show them what God has done and tell them the Good News about Jesus. Here are three important factors as you "show and tell" your friends about Jesus.

1. EARN THE RIGHT TO BE HEARD.

Before you evangelize with your words, you first need to demonstrate to your friends that they are important to you. We must see people as valuable, precious, made in the image of God. Every person you meet is so important to God that He sent Jesus to die for him or her – no matter his or her race, gender, religion, nationality, political views, sexual orientation, criminal record, and so forth .

If you really believe every person is loved by God, who is longing for relationship with him or her, it changes the way you treat that person. If we don't really care about people, but just tell them about Jesus out of obligation, they'll see through it. They likely won't be receptive to your message, because they'll probably feel more like an item on your to-do list that you just checked off, rather than a person you love.

I encourage you to be authentic with your friends. Love them out of the well of God's love that's in you. In this way, they'll see Jesus in you. Don't pretend that you've got life all together, that you never struggle. Be real, transparent.

You are not God, you are His vessel. And his light can shine through your "cracks" – your imperfections. Paul gives us a wonderful analogy in 2 Corinthians 4:7 (*NLT*), "We now have this light shining in our hearts, but we ourselves are like fragile clay jars containing this great treasure. This makes it clear that our great power is from God, not from ourselves."

The entire chapter of 2 Corinthians 4 is so good, I encourage you to read it all. The light that Paul describes is the message of Jesus that he preached to the Corinthians and to many thousands of others throughout Asia. He encourages us in this chapter to be real and truthful as we live out and share the Good News of Jesus.

2. SHOW JESUS TO YOUR FRIENDS.

Who is God bringing to your mind that doesn't yet know Jesus? I hope you can picture a few faces. These individuals need to see that you love them enough to show them Jesus. We show people Jesus by the way we live and the love we demonstrate to others.

God makes it crystal clear that we must love other believers if the world is ever going to believe that we know Jesus. Jesus said in John 13:34-35 (*NLT*), "So now I am giving you a new commandment: Love each other. Just as I have loved you, you should love each other. Your love for one another will prove to the world that you are my disciples."

There are times when it is really hard to obey Jesus' command. Sometimes our deepest wounds in relationships can come from people in the family of God. And God calls us to love like Jesus did. Jesus' love is sacrificial, it's repetitive, it's unconditional, and it's not the world's love.

Loving other Christians means forgiving even when we're deeply hurt. It means wishing the best for someone instead of competing with them. It means honoring and submitting to those in leadership over you. It means praying for other Christians, grieving with them, rejoicing with them, and living in accountability with each other. It means growing in God's Word together, even with people who annoy you or whom you don't really like.

It's this kind of community, mutual sacrifice, and maturity that makes the unbelieving world take notice and see Jesus. We are, after all, called the body of Christ, His church, of which

He is head. In Ephesians 4:15 (*NLT*), Paul gives us a vision of what it's like to live in unity and maturity, "...we will speak the truth in love, growing in every way more and more like Christ, who is the head of his body, the church."

Is this what your Christian community looks like? If not, I encourage you to pray that God will show you how to live like this. Be willing to make some changes in your life, either calling your friends into a deeper maturity, or possibly even seeing out different friendships or groups. But don't do this rashly; ask God for His direction and His plan.

Not only are we called to love Christians well, we are called to love our enemies. These "enemies" can be people who don't know Jesus yet and are still enemies of God, people in the church who have hurt you, or those who are just plain hard to get along with.

Jesus taught us in Luke 6:35 (*NLT*): "Love your enemies! Do good to them. Lend to them without expecting to be repaid. Then your reward from heaven will be very great, and you will truly be acting as children of the Most High, for he is kind to those who are unthankful and wicked."

3. TELL YOUR FRIENDS ABOUT JESUS.

Just as Jesus shared the Father with people, we need to share Him in both word and deed. Sharing your personal testimony is a great way to tell others about Jesus.

After I gave my life to Jesus at the age of 17, I wanted to tell all my friends about Jesus. My closest friend, Pat, and I played sports together. I invited him to church with me, and he came a few times.

One day, I told him about Jesus as I shared my testimony with him. Pat didn't want to begin a relationship with Jesus after I shared. I was so sad for him. That was over 24 years ago, and though I haven't kept in touch with him, I still pray for my friend Pat.

Being a witness for Jesus isn't easy, and many times, your friends will reject Jesus. But we are called to keep loving and telling others about Jesus. We must never give up, because God never gives up on us.

Let's pray.

Abba, Father, You made a way for us to live! You made a new and living way for us to come into Your presence through Your Son Jesus Christ. It's hard to imagine allowing someone I love to die for an enemy, but that's what You did. You sent Jesus to serve my death sentence when I was Your enemy.

Only He could do it, since He was the only One who didn't deserve that same sentence. He was the sinless, spotless, Lamb of God who takes away the sins of the world.

Help me to take that in – the gravity of Your sacrifice as a Father, and the sacrifice of Jesus Himself. No one took His life from Him, He laid it down willingly.

Abba, please forgive me for the times I have been ashamed of your gospel. Please forgive me for the times I have hardened my heart against members of Your body and failed to love them the way You do. Please forgive me for the times I have hated my enemies and cursed them instead of praying for them and blessing them.

Please help me to live a new way. Help me to share Your Good News with joy, because it is a privilege to do Your will and share Your blessing and salvation with those who are perishing. Please help me to see people the way you do – holy and dearly loved brothers and sisters or lost sheep whom You are earnestly seeking. Please use me to share Jesus with the world. In Jesus' Name, Amen.

THE HEART OF
THE SAVIOR

I love my wife Carmen! We have been married for seventeen years! The Lord has blessed Carmen and me with three beautiful children: Azlan, Mylie, and Tobin. My love for my family is intense, and I cannot imagine my life without them.

If I were ever faced with the choice of allowing my son to die in order to save someone else's life, I don't think I could do it. Yet, that is exactly what God did for you and me by sending His Son Jesus to die on the cross for our sins. Then, God raised Jesus from the grave.

God loves lost people. In Luke 19:10 Jesus said, "For the Son of Man came to seek and to save what was lost." If we want to bring our friends to Jesus, we need a heart like Jesus.

Jesus' heart was filled with love for the lost. As His followers, we need to have hearts that are filled with love for God and people. The Apostle Paul beautifully articulates and paints this picture in 2 Corinthians 5:14-21:

> *For Christ's love compels us, because we are convinced that one died for all, and therefore all died. And he died for*

all, that those who live should no longer live for themselves but for him who died for them and was raised again.

So from now on we regard no one from a worldly point of view. Though we once regarded Christ in this way, we do so no longer. Therefore, if anyone is in Christ, he is a new creation; the old has gone, the new has come! All this is from God, who reconciled us to himself through Christ and gave us the ministry of reconciliation: that God was reconciling the world to himself in Christ, not counting men's sins against them. And he has committed to us the message of reconciliation. We are therefore Christ's ambassadors, as though God were making his appeal through us. We implore you on Christ's behalf: Be reconciled to God. God made him who had no sin to be sin for us, so that in him we might become the righteousness of God.

How exciting is this? God has given us the privilege of being Christ's ambassadors and the ministry of reconciliation. We get to help people who are separated from God enter into a restored relationship with Him! We get to see people who were dead in sin become new creations! How awesome!

I'll say it again, evangelism is simple – fall so deeply in love with Jesus that you can't help but tell others about Him. Having a heart like Jesus is all about His love for us, our love for Him, and allowing the Holy Spirit to give us Christ-like love for the lost.

ZACCHAEUS THE TAX COLLECTOR

One of my favorite stories in the Bible is Jesus' encounter with Zacchaeus. This passage of Scripture gives us a clear picture of Jesus' love for the lost (*NLT*, Luke 19:1-10):

Jesus entered Jericho and made his way through the town. There was a man there named Zacchaeus. He was the chief tax collector in the region, and he had become very rich. He tried to get a look at Jesus, but he was too short to see over the crowd. So he ran ahead and climbed a sycamore-fig tree beside the road, for Jesus was going to pass that way.

When Jesus came by, he looked up at Zacchaeus and called him by name. "Zacchaeus!" he said. "Quick, come down! I must be a guest in your home today."

Zacchaeus quickly climbed down and took Jesus to his house in great excitement and joy. But the people were displeased. "He has gone to be the guest of a notorious sinner," they grumbled.

Meanwhile, Zacchaeus stood before the Lord and said, "I will give half my wealth to the poor, Lord, and if I have cheated people on their taxes, I will give them back four times as much!"

Jesus responded, "Salvation has come to this home today, for this man has shown himself to be a true son of Abraham. For the Son of Man came to seek and save those who are lost."

If you were to meet Zacchaeus on the road more than 2,000 years ago, you may have thought to yourself, "This guy has it all together." He was rich, dressed in fine clothes, and had the Roman government backing him up. As a chief tax collector, he made good money.

The problem was that he made his money by stealing from the people. It was the practice of tax collectors in that day to collect taxes from their own people (Jews), give Rome their portion, and keep the rest for themselves.

Zacchaeus may have looked good on the outside, but on the inside, he was corrupt, broken, and guilty. He probably didn't have many friends, if any, as a result of his reputation of ripping people off and working for the enemy, Rome.

One day, Zacchaeus learned that Jesus was coming to visit his town. There was something about Jesus that plucked at Zacchaeus' heart strings. He had likely heard about the miracles Jesus was performing: making the blind see, the lame walk, the deaf hear. Yes, there was something about Jesus that was like a magnet drawing Zacchaeus to Him. There was one big problem that Zacchaeus faced. Let's just say the local basketball team was not recruiting Zacchaeus to play for them.

The crowds were pressing in as Jesus entered Jericho. I imagine Zacchaeus was on his tip toes or even jumping to try and get a glimpse of Jesus. I can't help but laugh at what he did next. Because of the crowd, Zacchaeus ended up climbing a tree so he could see Jesus!

I love this! When God is working on a heart, there is nothing that can keep it from Him. God placed a longing in Zacchaeus so that he stopped at nothing to see the Savior. Can you imagine the scene? I bet kids were tugging on their moms' sleeves saying, "Look Mom! That rich tax collector, Zacchaeus, is climbing a tree!"

I imagine the mom saying, "Yes, it is strange, but there is no way I'm letting you climb up there with him!" Then something amazing took place. Zacchaeus was looking for Jesus and so wanted to see Him that he was willing to humble himself to climb a tree. But all along, Jesus was looking for Zacchaeus.

Did you catch that? All along Jesus was looking for Zacchaeus. "For the Son of Man came to seek and save those who are lost" (Luke 19:10).

Jesus approached the tree and called him by name, "Zacchaeus." Like honey in your mouth, it is so sweet to hear Jesus call your name. I imagine Zacchaeus' heart softened when he heard Jesus call him. Not only did Jesus call him by name, but He wanted to spend time with him! "Quick, come down! I must be a guest in your home today," (Luke 19:5).

Jesus changes everything! Zacchaeus went from broken to restored, from sinner to forgiven, from lonely to loved. The people were confused and even angry that of all the people, Jesus would choose to spend his lunch time with a sinner; and not just a sinner, but a chief sinner (or chief tax collector)!

But Jesus loves lost people. And from the way Zacchaeus responded after spending time with Jesus, he loved Jesus back. Jesus changed Zacchaeus life from the inside out, showing us what it looks like for a person to be in Christ, and a new creation (see 2 Corinthians 5:17).

This is the heart of the Savior – to heal, to redeem, to love, to forgive, to renew. Jesus alone is the hope of the world! There are many people like Zacchaeus in your community who look successful, but inside are longing to know Jesus and be made new.

Many years ago, there was a man riding home one evening in a horse-drawn carriage. The carriage driver looked up into the night sky and saw a meteorite shower. The carriage driver became very frightened, pulled the horse's reigns suddenly, and said, "It's the end of the world! It's the end of the world!"

The passenger hurried out of the carriage and looked into the sky. He calmed the driver, saying, "Don't worry or be frightened. Do you see that star way off in the distance? That's the North Star. Even if all the other stars fall, that one will remain. Keep your eyes on that star and we'll get home safely!"

We may be living in a crazy world, but that One star that lights this dark world and offers us hope is Jesus! He is the author of our faith, and we are called to fix our eyes on Him and run the race God has set before us (see Hebrews 12:2).

I wonder what became of Zacchaeus. I imagine God used him to reach many people in his town for Jesus. Probably every person that received stolen money back from Zacchaeus wanted to follow Jesus after witnessing the transformation of the tax collector.

How about you? Has Jesus called your name? If He is your Savior, then the answer is yes. Is there evidence in your life that you belong to Jesus? Are you living in a way that shows that you are a new creation?

It's time for us to get out of the tree, let Jesus into our house, and start living out the ministry of reconciliation God has entrusted to us, starting with our loved ones. Heaven and Hell is at stake. We only have one life to live. I'll close this chapter with the following poem:

"The Clock of Life"

Robert H. Smith, ©1932-1982

"The clock of life is wound but once,
And no man has the power
To tell just when the hands will stop
At late or early hour.

To lose one's wealth is sad indeed,
To lose one's health is more,
To lose one's soul is such a loss
That no man can restore.

The present only is our own,
So live, love, toil with a will,
Place no faith in "Tomorrow,"
For the Clock may then be still."

In the short time it took for you to read this poem, 39 people died. Every hour 5,417 die and enter into eternity. My dear friends, let's have the heart of our Savior to seek and love the lost and tell them about Jesus' gift of salvation!

Let's pray.

Lord Jesus, thank You for seeking me, calling my name, and making Your home in me. Please soften my heart and make it more like Yours. Help me to make the most of the time You've given me. In Your Name I pray, Amen.

part 2

TOOLS FOR SHARING YOUR FAITH

PRAY IN FAITH

I firmly believe that prayer is essential to evangelism. You and I don't save anyone. God does that work! That is why prayer is powerful and the most important part of being a contagious Christ-follower.

If we want God to save someone, we need to ask Him to allow us to be part of the process, and then get ready for Him to answer our prayers. And we need to pray, not just once, but continually, or without ceasing, as Paul directs us in 1 Thessalonians 5:17.

Paul gives more instruction on prayer in Colossians 4:2-6:

> *Devote yourselves to prayer, being watchful and thankful. And pray for us, too, that God may open a door for our message, so that we may proclaim the mystery of Christ, for which I am in chains. Pray that I may proclaim it clearly, as I should. Be wise in the way you act toward outsiders; make the most of every opportunity. Let your conversation be always full of grace, seasoned with salt, so that you may know how to answer everyone.*

We need to pray that God would soften the people in our lives to the Gospel. I remember growing up in Petaluma, California. Whenever I went and stayed at my grandparents' house, I would get up in the morning, go to the kitchen, and find my grandpa on his knees praying for me. When I was 17 years old, God answered my grandpa's prayers when I gave my life to Jesus Christ! Prayer is powerful.

One night after I preached the Good News of Jesus at an event, a man came up to me with tears in his eyes. He said, "Reid, for forty years I have prayed for my wife to give her life to Jesus. Tonight, God answered my prayers!" Wow! For forty years he prayed.

Often, people say to me, "Reid, you don't know my loved one. They have made so many poor decisions they won't ever come to Jesus." It breaks my heart when I hear those words, because God can soften the hardest of hearts.

We never give up on people, because we never give up on God. Don't ever give up. Keep praying like my grandpa prayed for me and like that husband prayed for his wife. Someone once said, "God moves in a mighty way when His people pray." James 5:16 says, "The prayer of a righteous person is powerful and effective."

Prayer moves mountains, and we need to get on our knees and pray to God for the souls of our friends that need Jesus.

I hope that you have seen the power of prayer in your own life and in the lives of those around you. I trust that as you pray now and in the future, you will see God work in powerful ways to answer your prayers.

Charles Swindoll told a story in his book Swindoll's Ultimate Book of Illustrations and Quotes (499-500):

> *Dick Russell had a Bible study group. An unsaved man, at the urging of his wife, joined the group and discovered he really liked the acceptance he found there and especially the prayer time. He realized even Christian men had*

serious issues to deal with in their lives, and week after week there were praises to God for answered prayer. No stranger to family problems, the man told Dick as he called one night, 'You know, my son was shot in the eye with a pellet gun. And the damage on the retina seems to be threatening his eyesight. I'd like you to pray, Dick, that God would restore the sight.' And so he agreed with him and they began to pray.

The next day, the doctor went in and discovered two cataracts, one on each eye, along with the damage in the retina. The fella was on his face before God as the doctor was doing his work. Then, lo and behold, when the gentlemen came home from the surgery, their house had been burglarized. And things were in a turmoil. He called Dick. Again they prayed. The operation was a miraculous success. His son was fitted with contacts, and he had his eyesight back.

Before long the phone rang again. Dick was asked to pray about another need. The fella's daughter, hooked on heroin, was becoming destructive and breaking the windows and destroying pieces of furniture in the home. He said to Dick, 'You have no idea what it's like to literally wrestle with your child and to pull her arms behind her back while the police snap the handcuffs on and take her out of the house.' That, by the way, led to harassment from the drug crowd that she was running with-motorcycle gangs and obscene phone calls and again attempted damage to the home. Just one breaking experience after another.

And the fella stayed in this Bible study. Dick prayed with him about this impossible situation, growing in urgency, but unknown to the people he worked with. Just sort of a quiet burden he held on to. Finally, this led to the ultimate. There was one person in the family with whom he really felt close, his wife's mother. And would you believe it, she had a heart attack. Just sort of an ultimate climax-a final blow.

That evening, he came home from work, went upstairs to his room without a word, and closed the door. His wife, downstairs fixing supper, heard a noise, heard words. She went up and listened. She heard this man, broken, weeping, just dumping out to the Lord every ugly sin in his life and saying, 'I'm spiritually bankrupt. I ask you now Father, through Jesus Christ, to come into my life.' And the wife, on the other side of the door, also wept, rejoicing at what God had done in this strange set of circumstances that broke that man to the place of submission and salvation. An answer to her own prayers for his salvation.

It's so encouraging to read this story and know that God is working to answer our prayers, even if we can't see it. Sometimes His answers are not what we expect, through circumstances we don't like, or in ways that don't fit with our plans or ideas.

When we pray and ask God, we also need to surrender to Him. We choose to trust that He sees everything, He knows the person we're praying for better than we do. He has a plan for that person that we may know nothing about. So pray continually, knowing that God "is able, through his mighty power at work within us, to accomplish infinitely more than we might ask or think," (*NLT*, Ephesians 3:20).

First, ask Jesus to give you His heart and love for the lost. Ask the Spirit of God to give you boldness to share the Gospel with your friends. Zechariah 4:6 says, "This is the word of the Lord to Zerubbabel: 'Not by might nor by power, but by my Spirit, says the Lord Almighty.'"

The Apostle Paul wrote in Ephesians 6:19-20, "Pray also for me, that whenever I open my mouth, words may be given me so that I will fearlessly make known the mystery of the Gospel, for which I am an ambassador in chains. Pray that I may declare it fearlessly, as I should."

Pray and ask God to give you an open door to share the Good News of Jesus with your family and friends. I firmly believe, and have seen firsthand, that when you give God an open heart, He will give you an open door to tell others about Jesus.

Second, I encourage you to write down on a piece of paper or in the notes section of your smart phone or tablet the names of three to five friends that you know who don't know Jesus. I call this the "Good News List." If you write this list on paper, put it where you'll see it daily to help remind you to pray every day. Some ideas are: on your bathroom mirror, as a bookmark in your Bible, or on your desk. If you have your list in your phone or tablet, you may wish to set a reminder that will pop up on your device every day at the same time.

This list can be anyone you know who needs Jesus. It could be a family member, friend, class mate, coworker, or neighbor. I want to challenge and encourage you to pray for them daily for the next three months. Pray that God would work on their hearts and draw them to Jesus.

I love what Hudson Taylor, the famous missionary to China, said: "Over the past forty years, the sun has never risen in China without finding me on my knees praying." What amazing discipline and devotion Mr. Taylor had for the Chinese people! What could happen if you and I would pray like that for the people we love?

We can have confidence that when we pray, God hears us. First Peter 3:12 is one of many passages that give us this assurance: "For the eyes of the Lord are on the righteous and His ears are attentive to their prayers."

So, pray daily for the three to five people on your "Good News List" and ask God to prepare their hearts for the Gospel.

One day I received a call from a man who asked me to come share Jesus with his dying dad. He told me, "Reid, I have been praying for years for my Dad to come to Jesus. He is going to die any day. Will you please come share Jesus with my dad?"

When I arrived at the man's house he introduced me to his dad, who was sitting in a wheelchair. He said, "Dad, you know how much I love you. I have been praying for years for you to know Jesus. I've invited my friend Reid to talk with you." The man then walked to the corner of the room and got on his knees to pray.

I turned to the dad and said, "Your son loves you very much. Jesus has changed your son's life for eternity. Would it be okay for me to tell you how Jesus can change your life?"

He nodded and said, "Yes."

Then, I explained the Good News that Jesus died on the cross for his sins and rose again from the dead. I quoted 2 Corinthians 5:21, "God made Him who had no sin to be sin for us, so that in Him we might become the righteousness of God." At that point, the dad prayed with me to give his life to Jesus.

It was truly a picture from heaven and the son ran up and embraced his dad. Both of them were in tears, rejoicing that they both knew Jesus and would see each other in heaven!

Keep praying and asking God for open doors to share the Good News with those on your "Good News List." I invite you to pray this prayer written by W. Gardiner-Hunter:

> *Dear Lord, I ask for the eyes that see deep down to the world's sore need, I ask for a love that holds nothing back, but pours out itself indeed; I want the passionate power of prayer that yearns for the great crowd's soul, I want to go among the fainting sheep and tell them my Lord makes whole. Let me look at the crowd as my Savior did, till my eyes with tears grow dim; let me look till I pity the wandering sheep, and love them for love of Him.*

THE BIBLE IS ALIVE!

In 2006, our team was ministering in Poland. I'll never forget a taxi driver named Stan that I met on this mission trip. I'm always looking for opportunities to share Jesus with others so when I got in Stan's taxi I started a conversation with him. With the help of an interpreter, I told Stan why our team was there – to bring the Good News of Jesus to the precious people of Poland. Stan told me he was religious, but I could quickly tell as we talked that he did not have a personal relationship with Jesus.

I shared the Good News of Jesus with Stan and quoted from John 3:16. "For God so loved the world that he gave his one and only Son, that whoever believes in him shall not perish but have eternal life."

Stan replied, "Those words are like honey to my heart."

Stan pulled his taxi to the side of the road and prayed with me to begin a person relationship with Jesus!

In all my years of sharing the Gospel, never have I heard such a wonderful response, describing the sweetness and power of God's Word to someone who is hungry for Him. The Bible is our authority to proclaim the Gospel to those in need of Jesus. God's Word is powerful!

The Bible is the sword of the Spirit and only weapon described in the full armor of God – all the other parts are for defense (see Ephesians 6:10-18). Some have argued that the Scriptures are a collection of writings from human authors. However, we get a different explanation from God.

First Peter 1:20-21 says, "Above all, you must understand that no prophecy of Scripture came about by the prophet's own interpretation. For prophecy never had its origin in the will of man, but men spoke from God as they were carried along by the Holy Spirit." The Bible was written by humans, but they were inspired by God's Sprit as they wrote. Therefore, the words of Scripture have the authority of God and we can trust them completely.

Second Timothy 3:16-17 declares, "All Scripture is God-breathed and is useful for teaching, rebuking, correcting and training in righteousness, so that the man of God may be thoroughly equipped for every good work." The Bible is not only inspired by God, but it is practical. God encourages us to use it as a tool to teach others about Him. As you share the Good News of Jesus with people, always use God's Word to share the message of Jesus. You're not just sharing your ideas about God, you're sharing God's own revelation of His plan of salvation.

Romans 10:17 says, "Faith comes from hearing the message, and the message is heard through the word of Christ." You and I do not save anyone. God does the saving; however, He has called us to share His message and love with the lost.

Hebrews 4:12 states, "For the word of God is living and active. Sharper than any double-edged sword, it penetrates even to dividing soul and spirit, joints and marrow; it judges the thoughts and attitudes of the heart." You and I can trust that as we speak God's Word, the Holy Spirit uses the Word to convict people of their sins and draw them to the Savior.

These verses in 1 Peter, 2 Timothy, Romans, and Hebrews give us good reason to take the Bible seriously. It is elevated above every book, every teaching, and every thought. The Bible is our sword and the standard by which we measure our lives.

If the Bible is that important to us, then it is also critical for us to be familiar with it so that we can wield it like a sword. No warrior goes into battle with a blade untested. He spends time in his armor, practicing his swordplay, long before he steps onto a battlefield. And trust me, friends, sharing the Gospel of Christ is entering the spiritual war that Satan and his demons have waged on the earth for thousands of years and will continue until he is locked up!

So, I encourage you to read the Bible daily as part of your routine. Start with prayer, thanking and praising God for who He is and for what He has done for you. Ask Him to help you understand His word and let it change how you think and live. There are websites and apps if you want to listen to God's Word instead of read it. (See the resources in Section 3 for links.)

However you do it, plug into God's Word every day. There are reading plans online and countless free tools and resources you can use to make this as practical and easy as possible. The main thing is that you discipline yourself to do it regularly. You will learn so much as you get to know God in the pages of Scripture and see who He is in history. He is the same today, so you can have confidence that He will keep the promises He made thousands of years ago. You'll see His faithfulness evidenced time and again in the stories you read from Genesis through Revelation.

Another practice I highly encourage you to develop is Scripture memorization. It's like swordplay for a warrior. You need to learn and memorize God's Word (in context) so that in the time of sharing your faith you can recall it easily and use it with confidence and strength.

I'll give you some recommended verses to memorize in the next chapter, but for now, let's pray.

> *God, thank You for Your Word. I want to know it more. I want to eat it like my food and drink it in like water. Your Word is breathed by Your Spirit, and I want to take it into the core of who I am and let it take root in me.*
>
> *Holy Spirit, please help me to understand Your Word more deeply and apply it to my everyday life. Please show me verses that I need to memorize and cling to during times of testing and temptation. Show me examples of people in Scripture that you are calling me to be like. Please help me to be bold and to share Scriptures with others, to teach, rebuke, correct, and train in righteousness.*
>
> *You are good, and Your Word is good, living, and active. Thank You for revealing Yourself and Your Son to me and the world through the Bible. In Jesus' Name, Amen.*

(Note: You can read the full version of Stan's story and see photos of him and our trip to Poland in *Stories from the Ends of the Earth*, 78-83).

chapter 9

SHARING THE GOSPEL WITH ACTIVE8

I don't bring my Bible with me everywhere I go, but it is amazing how the Spirit of God brings His Word to mind when I have an opportunity to share the Good News of Jesus with someone. If you want to effectively share your faith, make it a life practice to memorize Bible verses that clearly explain the Gospel.

A great place to start memorizing is Active8, which I listed for you in chapter 1. These verses from the book of Romans are like a road to salvation.

How are you doing on your memorization? I encourage you to keep working on it, and refresh your memory every few months so you don't forget them. Remember to pray that God will give you opportunities to share these verses with someone, like walking someone down a road to meeting Jesus. You can find the Active8 verses in chapter 1 or verse cards in section 3.

In my words, this is what Active8 teaches us: All of us share the same problem, we are sinful and separated from our glorious Creator. But by faith, we can be made right with God. God proves that He loves us; He sent Jesus to die for us when we were still in our sin. Our sin earned us death, and ultimately hell. But God gives us something we don't deserve, a free gift, of eternal life through Jesus. Anyone who receives Christ is free from accusation – all guilt is cleared! For anyone who believes and professes the truth that Jesus rose from the dead and is Lord, he or she is saved, free from sin and death!

Active8 is a tool for you, so I encourage you to become so familiar with these eight verses that you not only memorize them, but you can also explain them in your own words. If you can, try to determine the biblical knowledge of the person with whom you share. If they don't know much about the Bible, you may want to give them opportunities to ask questions; and keep your explanations pretty basic. I hope that God gives you opportunities to share Active8 with many different people with various life experiences.

Once you have a good grasp of Active8, I encourage you to get to know other ways to explain the Good News. There are more ideas for you in chapter nine, and more Scripture references in Section Three. For now, let's move forward as you prepare and pray for God to open a door to share Active8 with someone in your life.

WHAT MUST I DO TO BECOME A CHRISTIAN?

You might be thinking, "How do I explain what someone needs to do to become a follower of Christ?" Here is a clear, time-tested way that I have used to lead many people into a personal relationship with Jesus Christ.

1. **Repent**: this word literally means to "change your mind." When we repent, we are changing our mind about who and what we are trusting in for salvation. We see our sins as a barrier between us and a Holy God. We see Jesus as the only One qualified to remove that barrier. "Repent, then,

and turn to God, so that your sins may be wiped out, that times of refreshing may come from the Lord" (Acts 3:19).

2. **Respond**: by faith. Faith means to believe in what you cannot see, or to put your whole weight onto the object of your faith by trusting. It is okay to not understand everything. God knows your heart and He loves you. Romans 10:9-10 says, "If you confess with your mouth, 'Jesus is Lord,' and believe in your heart that God raised him from the dead, you will be saved. For it is with your heart that you believe and are justified (a big word that means 'just as if I'd never sinned'), and it is with your mouth that you confess and are saved."

3. **Receive**: it is not enough to know about God in your head. You need to open your heart to him and receive his free gift of eternal life through faith in Jesus and his finished work on the cross. John 1:12 says, "Yet to all who received Him, to those who believed in His name, He gave the right to become children of God."

Maybe you are reading this book and you realize that you do not have a personal relationship with Jesus Christ. We live in uncertain times. Chaos surrounds us, from the economy to the crime on our streets. Broken marriages and relationships affect us all and there seems to be a sense of widespread hopelessness in our world. Despite all the pain and suffering, I believe that God has not abandoned us. He is still working amidst the storms of life, and only He can bring lasting peace.

PRAYER OF DECISION

Think of it! Right now you can become a child of God and a part of His family! You can begin a personal relationship with Jesus Christ by praying to God. This prayer doesn't save you; your faith in Jesus does, but it merely confirms the decision you have just made in your heart.

Pray this right now.

> *Dear God, I know that I am have sinned. I have done and said things that have hurt You and others. I turn to You in faith, believing that You sent Your Son, Jesus Christ, to pay the debt for my sins when He died on the cross. I believe that three days later Jesus rose from the dead. Come into my heart, Lord Jesus. Forgive me of my sins. I receive your free gift of eternal life through faith in Jesus right now. In His Name I pray, Amen.*

If you just prayed that prayer, asking forgiveness and confessing your faith in Jesus, you are now part of the family of God. This is the first step in living your life all for Jesus! Now you can serve Jesus for the rest of your life, not because you have to, but because you are grateful for this free gift of eternal life through faith in Jesus Christ!

Perhaps you shared this prayer with someone else, who prayed and received Christ for the first time.

Whether it was you or someone you know, I am so excited for you (and him or her)! This is just the beginning of a life-long adventure of knowing God more and experiencing His restoration and love at work in you and those around you.

I would love to hear from you! Please write to me and tell me your story. I would love to send you a free gift to help you grow in your relationship with Christ. You can write me at Reid Saunders Association; PO Box 4275; Salem, OR 97302.

Let's pray.

> *Lord, thank You for revealing Your plan of salvation through the pages of Scripture. Please help us to receive Your plan, Your Son, Your forgiveness. Help us receive the joys and the trials you plan and allow in our lives.*
>
> *For my brothers and sisters who prayed the prayer of decision for the first time, THANK YOU! Thank you for their faith, and thank you for your mercy. Please protect them and help them to grow deep roots in Your love, Your Word, and Your family as they mature in Christ.*
>
> *Your Word is alive and active, so help us to commit ourselves to memorizing it and sharing it with others so that they can hear and believe too. And may we see Your Word bear fruit in the lives of those with whom we share.*
>
> *Please give us opportunities to share Active8, and help us to be aware when you do. Help us to be bold and led by Your Spirit, and always, to speak the truth in Your love. In Jesus' Name, Amen.*

chapter 10

TWO MORE WAYS TO SHARE

As followers of Jesus, we need to be prepared to share the Good News of Jesus when He gives us an opportunity! Peter encouraged believers, "But in your hearts set apart Christ as Lord. Always be prepared to give an answer to everyone who asks you to give the reason for the hope that you have. But do this with gentleness and respect..." (1 Peter 3:15).

A few years ago, I needed to put a lawn in my back yard. I couldn't do it by myself so I hired a man named John. For a week as we put in the lawn I built a friendship with John and prayed daily for him to come to Jesus.

As we finished the project, John and I were standing in my driveway. I said, "John, you know I love Jesus and that He changed my life. Would it be okay if I tell you how Jesus can change your life?"

I love seeing the Holy Spirit get ahold of a heart. John looked at me and said, "I have been around you for a week, and I want what you have." Right there in my driveway, I told John the Good News and he gave his life to Jesus Christ! Praise

God! If you are walking with Jesus, then there are people in your life that want what you have, too!

At the conclusion of the book of Acts, Paul is in custody in Rome. And in those tough circumstances, Paul made the most of his time! "For two whole years Paul stayed there in his own rented house and welcomed all who came to see him. Boldly and without hindrance he preached the kingdom of God and taught about the Lord Jesus Christ" (Acts 28:30-31).

Notice how Paul shared about Jesus – **boldly** and **without hindrance**. Paul had already suffered many times for sharing the Good News, but he had no fear of continuing to do so. He knew the Gospel was the power of God and he didn't let anything keep him from sharing it. What an example for us to follow!

Remember, you can do all things through Christ who gives you strength, and with Him all things are possible. Successful witnessing means taking the initiative by the power of the Holy Spirit and leaving the results to God! The following is a sample four-point outline you can use for presenting the Gospel. It is similar to the Four Spiritual Laws, developed by Cru. (To read or purchase Cru's tracts, go to http://crustore.org/fourlawseng.htm.)

Remember, it's not a script, just a starting point. Just like with Active8, I encourage you to memorize the Scripture passages, read and understand them in context, and become familiar with the ideas behind each one. With any Scripture memorization, you may find it helpful to use index cards.

HOW TO KNOW JESUS CHRIST

1. GOD'S PLAN – PEACE AND LIFE

God wants a personal relationship with you. The Bible speaks of God's great love for you and His desire to give you eternal life in heaven. "For God so loved the world that he gave his one and only Son, that whoever believes in him shall not perish but have eternal life" (John 3:16).

2. HUMANITY'S PROBLEM – SEPARATION AND JUDGMENT

Man is sinful by nature and has rejected God. The Bible says, "There is no one righteous, not even one; there is no one who understands, no one who seeks God. All have turned away, they have together become worthless; there is no one who does good, not even one" (Romans 3:10-12).

Because of our sinful condition, we stand guilty before God and deserve eternal condemnation. "He will punish those who do not know God and do not obey the gospel of our Lord Jesus. They will be punished with everlasting destruction and shut out from the presence of the Lord and from the majesty of his power...." (2 Thessalonians 1:8-9).

3. GOD'S REMEDY – JESUS CHRIST

God the Father sent Jesus, His only Son, to be born of a virgin. Jesus, who was God in the flesh, lived a sinless life. He was crucified and died, taking our place and paying our penalty for sin. The Bible says, "God made Him who had no sin to be sin for us, so that in Him we might become the righteousness of God" (2 Corinthians 5:21).

Then Jesus ascended into heaven and sat at the right hand of God the Father. The Father has given Jesus all authority in heaven and on earth. He is King of kings and Lord of lords, and one day, He is coming back. He urges us to be ready for that day, which only the Father knows.

Remember, as we read earlier in this book, that presenting the biblical identity of Jesus Christ is critical as you share the Good News with someone. This is one of the reasons why it is so important for you to nurture your relationship with Him by spending time with Him and in His Word. Get to know and memorize key passages about His identity so that you can present Him accurately and answer questions that people may have.

4. OUR RESPONSE – RECEIVE JESUS CHRIST

God invites us to respond to His love by trusting Jesus Christ by faith, and not by our own effort. This means we accept Christ's death on the cross as payment for our sins and freely receive Him as Savior and Lord. "For it is by grace you have been saved, through faith – and this not from yourselves, it is the gift of God – not by works, so that no one can boast" (Ephesians 2:8-9).

By receiving Jesus, we become children of God. "Yet to all who received Him, to those who believed in his Name, he gave the right to become children of God...." (John 1:12).

After explaining the Gospel to someone, ask if they understand or have any questions. This will likely lead to more conversation. If the person is receptive, be bold and ask, "Would you like to pray to receive Jesus Christ today?"

If their answer is yes, you can use the same Prayer of Decision from the last chapter:

> *Dear God, I know that I am have sinned. I have done and said things that have hurt You and others. I turn to You in faith, believing that You sent Your Son, Jesus Christ, to pay the debt for my sins when He died on the cross. I believe that three days later Jesus rose from the dead. Come into my heart, Lord Jesus. Forgive me of my sins. I receive your free gift of eternal life through faith in Jesus right now. In His Name I pray, Amen.*

If their answer is no, you may want to ask "why not?" and continue the conversation. Or you may ask to pray for them. If they're willing, pray for them right then, asking the Father to draw them to Jesus and protect them from the evil one. And pray however else God leads you.

Continue to pray for that person and ask God to help you build, or continue, a relationship with that person in which you can help them grow in their faith.

HAND OF HOPE

Another tool that you can use to be a witness for Jesus is called the hand of hope. You take your hand as an illustration to go over five points of salvation from the thumb to the pinky.

1. THUMB

God made you for a relationship with Him. Jesus said in John 10:10, "...I have come that they may have life, and have it to the full."

2. POINTER FINGER

Sin separates you from God. Romans 3:23 says, "...for all have sinned and fall short of the glory of God." Isaiah 59:2 says, "But your iniquities have separated you from your God; your sins have hidden his face from you, so that He will not hear."

3. MIDDLE FINGER

Jesus died on the cross in your place for your sins and rose again from the grave. Romans 5:8 says, "But God demonstrates His own love for us in this: While we were still sinners, Christ died for us." Jesus gave His life for you that you may live.

We are saved because of Christ's free gift to us, not by anything we can do (see Ephesians 2:8-9).

4. RING FINGER

Jesus is the only way to heaven. When we die we either go to heaven or hell. Jesus said in John 14:6, "I am the way and the truth and the life. No one comes to the Father except through me." Acts 4:12 says about Jesus, "Salvation is found in no one else, for there is no other name under heaven given to men by which we must be saved."

5. PINKY

You need to make a decision to put your faith in Jesus. Romans 10:9-10 says, "That if you confess with your mouth, 'Jesus is Lord,' and believe in you heart that God raised Him from the dead, you will be saved. For it is with your heart that you believe and are justified, and it is with your mouth that you confess and are saved."

Again, follow up the Good News by allowing the person to ask questions or give feedback. Ask if they'd like to receive Jesus, and if so, lead them in a Prayer of Decision.

Let's pray together.

Father in Heaven, thank You for the Good News. Thank You for equipping me to share it with others who don't yet know You or Your Son. Please help me to be diligent to know and memorize passages from Your Word that explain Your plan of salvation.

Father, please open doors for the Gospel with people I know. I pray for family members, friends, and other people in my life who are separated from You. There is no heart too hard for You, no sin too great for You to redeem. Help me to pray and persevere, filled with Your hope and the power of Your Holy Spirit.

Please draw _____ (pray the names of your loved ones who aren't yet saved) to Jesus. Holy Spirit, convict them of their sin and their need for forgiveness and salvation through Christ. Please help them to believe in You and Your Son. In Jesus' Name, Amen.

SHARE YOUR STORY

On a flight from Washington, D.C. to Dallas, I noticed a businessman board the plane after me. His suit and hair were disheveled and he looked weary and stressed.

The man mumbled to himself as he stuffed his luggage in the overhead compartment and flung himself down into the middle seat a few rows behind me. Shortly, a fellow passenger came to his aisle and said, "Excuse me, but I believe you are sitting in my seat."

The businessman looked at his ticket and sighed. "Oh, I'm in the seat ahead. Can this day get any worse?" Then he moved one row forward.

Just as the man got settled in his new seat, another passenger came to his aisle, saying, "Pardon me, but I think you're in my seat."

At this point, the businessman let out a frustrated sigh, looked at his ticket again, and exclaimed: "Unbelievable! I'm in the wrong seat again! What a day!" Once again he grabbed his belongings and plopped down into his assigned seat, 14b, right next to me!

I'm always looking for opportunities to tell others about Jesus. First Peter 3:15 says, "But in your hearts set apart Christ as Lord. Always be prepared to give an answer to everyone who asks you to give the reason for the hope that you have. But do this with gentleness and respect."

When the businessman sat down next to me, I knew this was a time to be prepared. I introduced myself and learned the man's name was Joe. He told me all about his bad day, using words that would have been "bleeped" out on prime-time TV.

Then Joe asked me about myself. When he found out I was an evangelist, he was intrigued. He was amazed that I would spend my life traveling the world to tell people about Jesus. I asked Joe if he knew about Jesus and he told me he did not know much.

Seeing that he was open and interested, I shared my story, or testimony, to explain the Good News of Jesus to Joe. Although he did not choose to follow Jesus on the plane that day, I know seeds were planted in Joe's heart.

People often tell me about a fear that keeps them from sharing their faith with others. "What if I share the Gospel, but someone has tough questions that I can't answer?" Maybe as you are reading this book you are thinking the same thing. That is why telling your story is one of the greatest ways you can evangelize.

You are familiar with your life and testimony, so you can easily answer questions people ask you about it. And, your life experiences aren't really subject to debate like the Bible or other objective sources.

PAUL AND KING AGRIPPA

The Apostle Paul often used his testimony when he had an opportunity to share the Gospel. Let's read together about the time he was before King Agrippa (Acts 26:1-23):

Then Agrippa said to Paul, "You have permission to speak for yourself."

So Paul motioned with his hand and began his defense: "King Agrippa, I consider myself fortunate to stand before you today as I make my defense against all the accusations of the Jews, and especially so because you are well acquainted with all the Jewish customs and controversies. Therefore, I beg you to listen to me patiently.

"The Jews all know the way I have lived ever since I was a child, from the beginning of my life in my own country, and also in Jerusalem. They have known me for a long time and can testify, if they are willing, that according to the strictest sect of our religion, I lived as a Pharisee. And now it is because of my hope in what God has promised our fathers that I am on trial today. This is the promise our twelve tribes are hoping to see fulfilled as they earnestly serve God day and night. O King, it is because of this hope that the Jews are accusing me. Why should any of you consider it incredible that God raises the dead?

"I too was convinced that I ought to do all that was possible to oppose the name of Jesus of Nazareth. And that is just what I did in Jerusalem. On the authority of the chief priests I put many of the saints in prison, and when they were put to death, I cast my vote against them. Many a time I went from one synagogue to another to have them punished, and I tried to force them to blaspheme. In my obsession against them, I even went to foreign cities to persecute them.

"On one of these journeys I was going to Damascus with the authority and commission of the chief priests. About noon, O King, as I was on the road, I saw a light from heaven, brighter than the sun, blazing around me and my companions. We all fell to the ground, and I heard a voice saying to me in Aramaic, 'Saul, Saul, why do you persecute me? It is hard for you to kick against the goads.'

"Then I asked, 'Who are you, Lord?'

" 'I am Jesus, whom you are persecuting,' the Lord replied. 'Now get up and stand on your feet. I have appeared to you to appoint you as a servant and as a witness of what you have seen of me and what I will show you. I will rescue you from your own people and from the Gentiles. I am sending you to them to open their eyes and turn them from darkness to light, and from the power of Satan to God, so that they may receive forgiveness of sins and a place among those who are sanctified by faith in me.'

"So then, King Agrippa, I was not disobedient to the vision from heaven. First to those in Damascus, then to those in Jerusalem and in all Judea, and to the Gentiles also, I preached that they should repent and turn to God and prove their repentance by their deeds. That is why the Jews seized me in the temple courts and tried to kill me. But I have had God's help to this very day, and so I stand here and testify to small and great alike. I am saying nothing beyond what the prophets and Moses said would happen—that the Christ would suffer and, as the first to rise from the dead, would proclaim light to his own people and to the Gentiles."

If you have a hunger to become skilled at sharing your faith, study this passage in depth, as well as other passages where Paul explains the Gospel to different groups of people. The Gospel is always the same, but the way Paul presents it to different audiences is tailored for their culture, experiences, and understanding of the Scriptures.

In King Agrippa's case, Paul was speaking to a man in authority who understood Jewish customs. So Paul began his address to the King by honoring his position and his knowledge, then he spoke of his own upbringing and life as a Jew.

Paul spoke of his zeal in persecuting those who followed Jesus. Then he related his encounter with Christ, the turning point in his life where He humbled himself and became a Christian. Paul explained his journey of faith from that moment forward.

SHARING YOUR STORY

Paul is a great model for us as we seek to grow in our lifestyle of evangelism. You can break down your testimony in three simple steps.

Memorize your testimony and be prepared to share when God gives you an open door. Remember, when you give God an open heart He will give you an open door to share the Gospel.

BC-CC-WC is a great way to share your story with others. Here is a testimony outline you can use to get you started.

I encourage you right now to grab a note pad or use your smart phone to write out your testimony. Try to keep your testimony between three and five minutes when you say it.

BC = Before I accepted Christ

- What problems or feelings did you struggle with?
- What did your life revolve around?
- How did these things let you down?

CC = Commitment to Christ

- When was the first time I heard the Gospel?
- What were my initial reactions?
- When did my attitude begin to change? Why?

WC = Walking with Christ

- What are the specific changes Christ has made in your life?
- What has your life been like since becoming a Christian? Think through the benefits of knowing Christ.

Helpful hints:

Try to write the way you speak – make the testimony yours. Don't exaggerate or be overly dramatic – be truthful and genuine. Practice it over and over again until it becomes natural.

Remember, you are a vital part of the Great Commission and God wants to use your life to make a difference for eternity! It is very important to be transparent and real with people when you share your story. It is also good to prepare a longer testimony for the times you have to share with a friend, like at a coffee shop or in a home. As I've said before, evangelism is simple. Fall so deeply in love with Jesus that you can't help but tell others about Him.

JOANNA'S STORY

Several years ago, I was speaking at a youth camp when a girl came up to me with a group of her friends and said, "Are you the camp speaker?"

"Yes!" I said.

Joanna exclaimed. "Listen up. I don't believe in God or want anything to do with Him. So leave me alone!"

I began to pray and ask God to show His love to Joanna. The next day Joanna came up to me and said, "Reid, I woke up at four in the morning. I was shaking, shivering, and sweating. What is going on?"

I replied, "Don't eat the camp food!" Just kidding. I really told her, "Maybe God is trying to show you that He is real and loves you."

That night after I shared the Gospel message, Joanna prayed to receive Jesus. With tears in her eyes, she told me how excited she was to know Jesus. She had been in and out of foster homes her whole life and never felt truly loved. "Reid, for the first time in my life, I feel hope and love in my heart thanks to Jesus."

The camp ended on Saturday and the following Thursday there was a camp reunion where students could share their testimony with others. Joanna stood up and shared with everyone. "As you know, I gave my life to Jesus at camp. Jesus changed my life in such a powerful way I wanted all my friends to know about Jesus. Since camp, I shared my testimony with five of my friends and led them to Jesus!"

Awesome! I love how God can change and use someone like Joanna to make a difference for eternity! My prayer for you is that you will write out, memorize, and share your story with your friends! Then, you will be living out the Great Commission, and you will fully understand all the awesome blessings of Jesus. Paul puts it this way in one of the verses in Active8. "I pray that you may be active in sharing your faith, so that you will have a full understanding of every good thing we have in Christ" (Philemon 1:6).

MOSES FROM UGANDA

Even though I have shared Moses' story before in previous books, I want to share it here briefly. It is one of the most dramatic examples I have personally witnessed of someone receiving Christ and immediately beginning to share their faith with others.

Several years ago, when we were on a mission trip in Kayunga, Uganda, we met Moses. While we were doing a service project, one of our team members saw Moses working at a shop in the area and invited him to our upcoming festival.

Moses quickly declined, since he was a Muslim and understood that it was a festival with a Christian focus. Later that day our team had a soccer outreach, and we were very surprised that Moses was one of the soccer players in the match. At halftime, when I shared the gospel message, Moses responded to the Good News. His Muslim friends and teammates mocked him, but it did not sway him from his decision to follow Jesus.

This young man, who formerly went by a Muslim name, asked to be called Moses. When Moses' father learned of his son's conversion, he put all of Moses' belongings outside their house and told Moses to either renounce his faith in Jesus or his family.

Moses chose Jesus, and each day, Moses brought family members and friends to our lodging and our events so they could hear the Good News. Moses' mother, sisters, uncle, and friends, one by one, believed the message of salvation and received Christ.

At our festival, Moses shared his testimony on stage. He was understandably nervous, as Muslims in the community had made threats on his life. However, with the boldness of a lion, Moses told his story of having been a Muslim, believing in Jesus, and living for Him. That night, the friends who had mocked him at the soccer match, and who had threatened his life earlier that day, surrendered to Jesus.

Six days after meeting Moses, TWENTY-SIX of his family members and friends chose to follow Jesus. His father was not one of them, but we pray that either he did or will receive the Savior. We have since lost touch with Moses, but will you pray with us that wherever he is, he will walk with Jesus and keep telling his story?

Let's pray now.

Father in Heaven, THANK YOU. We are grateful that you have given us a story worth sharing. Our stories are not all neat little packages tied up in a bow. Some things are ugly, painful, and sometimes embarrassing. But our stories are also full of beauty, strength, and Your power to redeem our darkest moments, choices, and suffering.

Thank you for showing us Your story, and adopting us into it. You have written our story from beginning to end and you know everything about it, so much better than we do.

Help us to trust you more, giving you full reign over every part of our story. Help us not to be ashamed of our story, but to tell it in its truth and power. Please use our stories to help others see You and Your Son and Your Spirit. Use each of us to teach others what You are like and how You work in human lives.

Please use our stories to draw people to Jesus. And help us to see You in our story more and more, giving thanks to You for every way that You take the things Satan means for harm and turn it, using it for the salvation of many.

And we pray for Moses and Joanna to keep growing in Jesus and sharing their stories. In Jesus' Name, Amen.

(Note: You can read the full version of Moses' story and see photos of him and our team's ministry in Uganda in *Stories from the Ends of the Earth* (61-65).

chapter 12

THE HOLY SPIRIT IS OUR HELPER

I have a confession to make. I love watching the *Home Alone* movies. Yes, I'm a kid at heart and I laugh every time I watch Kevin take out the crooks, Harry and Marv. For some bonding and laughs, I decided it was time for my eight year old son, Azlan, to watch the first Home Alone movie with me. We both had a great time.

Later that night after I tucked Azlan into bed, I turned out the lights and started walking down the stairs. At the third step, I felt an intensely sharp pain that started from the sole of my foot and shot up to the top of my head. I screamed out in sheer pain! I turned on the light and pulled out a nail from my foot that had been strategically placed inside a piece of cardboard so the nail would stick straight up.

I was so angry! I knew it was Azlan, so I limped into his room. In my best Harry voice, I growled, "Azlan! Did you put a nail on the stairs?" Azlan bolted upright and said, wide-eyed, "Yes, Dad, I did it in case the bad guys Marv and Harry showed up! I wanted to protect our house from the bad guys like Kevin did!"

Movies, and the impression they leave on us, are powerful. Just ask my foot!

The Holy Spirit is even more powerful, and He is the One who powerfully works in and through us to reach people for Jesus. Zechariah 4:6 says, "This is the word of the Lord to Zerubbabel: 'Not by might nor by power, but by my Spirit,' says the Lord Almighty." The Holy Spirit, the Third Person of the Trinity, works in and through us to reach people for Jesus.

The famous evangelist D.L. Moody once said, "If you have been born of the Holy Spirit, you will not have to serve God... it will become the natural thing to do." As we strive to live our lives as Christ-followers, it is crucial that we live Spirit-filled and Spirit-led lives.

Even though we become sealed by the Holy Spirit the moment we receive Christ, we can choose to live in the Spirit or to live in our sinful nature. A.W. Tozer says, "Though every believer has the Holy Spirit, the Holy Spirit does not have every believer." We can even grieve the Holy Spirit by the things we say and do (or don't say and don't do) and make ourselves calloused to the Spirit's work in our lives.

As we yield our lives to Jesus, the Holy Spirit uses us to share the Good News of Jesus with passion and boldness. As I've stated before, you and I don't save people, The Holy Spirit does that work. Jesus gave His disciples a promise before He ascended to heaven: "But you will receive power when the Holy Spirit comes on you; and you will be my witnesses in Jerusalem, and in all Judea and Samaria, and to the ends of the earth."

This gets me excited! As we allow the Holy Spirit to use our lives as His vessels, He powerfully works in and through us to reach people for Jesus! Jesus describes the Holy Spirit to His disciples in John 16:7-11:

But I tell you the truth: It is for your good that I am going away. Unless I go away, the Counselor will not come to you; but if I go, I will send Him to you. When He comes, He will convict the world of guilt in regard to sin and righteousness and judgment: in regard to sin, because men do not believe in Me; in regard to righteousness, because I am going to the Father, where you can see me no longer; and in regard to judgment, because the prince of this world now stands condemned.

The Holy Spirit is both the Comforter and the One who convicts people of sin. He is working in our world and He wants to use your life to make a difference for eternity! Here are three ways I have found that the Holy Spirit can give you power to actively share your faith in Jesus with others:

1. THE POWER OF PRAYER

Pray daily for people you know who need Jesus. Ask the Holy Spirit to work in their hearts and give you an open door and an opportunity to share Jesus with them.

2. THE POWER OF AUTHORITY

Remember that as a follower of Jesus, you have His power and authority to preach His Gospel. When Jesus gave the Great Commission in Matthew 28:19-20, He began by telling His disciples that all authority in heaven and on earth had been given to Him. Jesus' authority is the basis for Him commissioning us, and giving us His authority to be His witnesses to the ends of the earth. Be encouraged that the Holy Spirit is powerfully working in you to share Jesus with others. You have His authority to share the Good News of Jesus! Exciting!

3. THE POWER OF HIS PRESENCE

Whenever I get up to preach the Good News of Jesus, I remember that the Holy Spirit is present. He is working and preparing hearts to respond to the Gospel! I love how, in Acts 4, the Holy Spirit gave great boldness and assurance of His presence in the work of evangelism to the disciples as they prayed. "Now, Lord, consider their threats and enable your servants to speak Your Word with great boldness.... After they prayed, the place where they were meeting was shaken. And they were all filled with the Holy Spirit and spoke the Word of God boldly" (Acts 4:29, 31).

Like the first disciples, I pray that you will find encouragement and boldness to share Jesus with others as you trust and rely on the presence and power of the Holy Spirit to work in and through you to reach people for Jesus Christ!

MARY'S STORY

As I have traveled the world preaching the Good News of Jesus, I have seen the Holy Spirit work in hearts to bring them to Jesus! In 2003 we held an evangelistic outreach in Masindi, Uganda.

It was a great time of sharing the Good News of Jesus at an outdoor festival, where thousands of people received the Lord. We were also holding small training events in friendship evangelism in remote churches located in the bush on the outskirts of Masindi. I had the privilege of speaking on the radio, sharing the Gospel and inviting people to come to one of these trainings where they could learn to share Christ with confidence.

One particular morning, our team was getting ready to head out for the day to minister at several of these trainings. But there was a problem. All the trainings had speakers except for one small church located far off in the African bush.

They asked me to go, but I planned to stay back to study and prepare for my message at the evening festival. I really didn't want to go, as it was a long drive in the jungle, and I was concerned about being too worn out for that evening's festival. However, I felt the Lord prompting me to go. He reminded me in my heart that these people needed Jesus.

I agreed to go and jumped into a van filled with pastors as we traveled through the bush. At one point one of the pastors shouted "Look! A king cobra just went underneath our van!" I almost passed out!

I said, "What? I hate snakes!" All the pastors laughed, threw back their heads and said, "Brother Reid. The African Bush is filled with the King Cobra!" Indiana Jones and I have one thing in common – we both hate snakes!

By faith, I stayed in the van and continued through the Bush to a remote village. In the only church in the village, I did the training and like always, I preached the Gospel and gave people an opportunity to receive Jesus as their personal Lord and Savior.

A lady named Mary stood and walked to the front. The Pastor spoke with her in their native language, and both of them started to cry. The Pastor then had the woman share her story with the people gathered. Like the angels in Luke 15 celebrated in heaven, those in the church rejoiced that Mary had come to Christ.

Mary shared with us how she had trouble sleeping the previous night. She was not a believer in Jesus. In fact, Mary wanted nothing to do with God. As she lay awake in the night, she felt God was urging her to turn on the radio. As soon as she turned on the radio she heard my voice announcing the training to be held at a church.

Mary felt that God was tugging at her heart, wanting her to go to this church. She wasn't sure how she would go, since the church was far from her home, but Mary said the pull on her heart was so strong that she decided she would go before falling asleep. Getting up early, Mary walked all morning to attend this training at the church.

Little did Mary, the pastor, or I know what a transformation would happen in her life that day. Isn't that exciting? I love how the Holy Spirit moved in Mary's heart, and mine, to bring us both to that training! When she came to Jesus, Mary was welcomed into the Body of Christ by a church family in the African bush.

Friends, the Holy Spirit works in mighty and powerful ways to bring people to Jesus! You and I have the joy and privilege of having the Holy Spirit live and work in us to reach our friends, family, neighbors, and co-workers for Jesus! That is what life is all about. It's all for Jesus!

Let's pray:

Jesus, thank You for sending Your Holy Spirit to us after You ascended to Heaven. Your Spirit has worked powerfully in my life.

Thank You for every time You have convicted me of sin. Thank You for counseling me and leading me when I need wisdom to make good decisions. Thank you for prompting me to reach out to others when I would not naturally do so.

Please forgive me for the times that my thoughts, words, and deeds have grieved Your Holy Spirit. Please forgive me for the times when I have ignored Your voice and Your leading.

I want to walk with You and trust You more intimately than I ever have before. Please help me to grow and to walk in step with You. In Jesus' Name, Amen.

MAKING DISCIPLES LIKE JESUS DID

Let's imagine for a moment that you have a newborn baby. After preparing for this child's birth for nine months, she has been born and there is no more waiting. What do you do next? Do you rejoice in the excitement of birth and leave the baby to raise herself?

Now you have a responsibility to this child to help her grow. You will feed her, bond with her, help her brain grow by reading to her and playing with her, help her body grow by letting her lay on her tummy and strengthen her neck muscles. And you will continue to care for her day in and day out, year after year, until she is mature and can care for herself and others.

If the Lord calls you to invest your life in others, to be poured out like a drink offering as Paul was, then why would you abandon someone just when their new life has begun? Why would you leave them to figure things out and grow up on their own when they need your support and prayers and encouragement as a believer just as much as they did before they believed?

Once a person receives Christ as Savior, they become your brother or sister in Christ. So, please, don't abandon your family. Stick with them through their journey of growth. It's an exciting time!

Pray for your friend or family member, keep in touch regularly, invite them to attend your church, small group, and/or Bible study. Include them in your family times. If they don't have a Bible yet, give them one (or get one for them from your church).

And for you, now you have an added motivation to keep growing in your faith. You've got a baby Christian watching you and learning from your example. If you don't have a mentor, pray for and seek out someone who can encourage you in your faith.

Keep your relationship with Jesus fresh by reading Scripture daily, praying throughout each day, and regularly spending time with other believers who show you by their lives and words that Jesus is alive!

Jesus did much more than give a command to His disciples and those who would become His disciples in the future. He modeled the Great Commission every day that He lived on earth. It is wise, therefore, to examine His life as recorded in the Gospels.

FIVE PHASES OF DISCIPLESHIP

I encourage you to read Luke 4 through Luke 11. If you don't mind highlighting and/or making notes in your Bible, use that. Or, you might want to photocopy your Bible or print out those chapters from a website such as www.biblegateway.com or a program like Logos Bible Software.

While you're reading and taking notes, think about how Jesus leads people in a progression of spiritual growth. In a class offered by Soul Thirst Disciple Making and Real Life Ministries, there are terms they use to describe five phases of the discipleship process:

1. ATTEND

Anyone who simply attends church, in the Gospels anyone who listened to Christ's teaching, falls into this broad category. There are two stages of an attender. Stage one is without Christ and stage two is accepting Christ. Examples: Luke 4:15, 22.

2. FOLLOW

A follower of Jesus is in the child stage of spiritual development. He or she is in a new commitment to church, mission, and vision but is not yet connected in deep, growing relationships in the body of Christ and is self-centered. Examples: Luke 5:11; 6:12-16

3. CONNECT

This person is connected in relational environment for the purpose of biblical discipleship. They are moving into the adolescent stage of spiritual development. Someone in this phase can get stuck in routines or groups and not want to change or include new people. Examples: Luke 8:1, 9-10

4. MINISTER

Someone in the ministry phase is a growing believer who is serving within the local church. This person takes guidance from their leaders, cares for the needs of others, and is other-centered. He or she is moving into the adult phase of spiritual maturity. Examples: Luke 9:1-5, 12-17; 10:1-24

5. MULTIPLY

Those who are in the adult phase of spiritual maturity, who have proven their faith over time in their way of living and relationships with others, are multipliers. They cultivate their own relationship with God, yet are very other-centered and intentional about serving. When they see weaknesses in others, they ask God how they can help train and encourage that person to grow. Examples: Matthew 28:16-20; Acts 2:42-47; 3:1-4:37

These five stages serve only as a seriously condensed ver-sion of a disciple making course I encourage you to attend. You can find more information at http://soulthirstdisciplemaking.com/ or http://www.reallifeministries.com/discipleshift1/. Another great resource for this type of training is Sonlife – http://www.sonlife.com/training-events/.

In the training offered by Soul Thirst, Real Life Ministries, or Sonlife, you'll look in-depth at how Jesus made disciples in the Gospels and the implications that has for you and me in the twenty-first century.

I hope that reading a summary of the five phases of discipleship helps as you think about sharing Jesus with people God has placed (and will place) in your life. It would be a great study for you to read through Luke 4-11, and eventually all four Gospels, and highlight these five phases. Take note of how Jesus related with people, especially with his closest disciples, the twelve.

After making careful observation of how Jesus made disciples, make it personal. What difference do the things you've learned make to you? Spend some time in prayer, asking the Holy Spirit to help you see ways that you need to change in the way you relate to others. Then, so that you remember what the Lord is showing you, write it down.

If you like to journal or draw, let your pen (or drawing utensil) flow. But then, I encourage you to use index cards or sticky notes to write a few words or one sentence each that will quickly jog your memory. Then put these cards or notes somewhere you'll see them when you need them most (in your locker at school, on your desk at work, on your mirror at home, in your car, as an example).

I realize this "assignment" is going to take you probably several hours. So I encourage you to break it down into manageable pieces. Maybe read one chapter a day and make notes. Make yourself a realistic goal. But please, do this. It will change you, your relationship with Jesus, and your relationship with others, if you really want it to and invest yourself in it.

My prayer for us:

Father, please help us to quiet ourselves. Silence the voice of our accuser and the worries and distractions that seek to choke out our faith. Holy Spirit, please speak to us. Help us to see this world the way you do, and to see ourselves and others the way you do.

Father, please draw us closer to Jesus. Let us drink in His Word, His attitude of humility, His life of service, His power to proclaim and to heal, His authority over the enemy, His teaching, His way of life. Let us meditate on the Gospels and observe with fresh eyes of faith how Jesus lived and shared His faith in You, and how it changed the world around Him... forever. In Jesus' Name, Amen.

EVANGELISM STYLES

My friend, Pastor Justin Greene, his son Brenden, my son Azlan, and I returned from a mission trip to Peru last year. We trained pastors as we prepared for a festival to follow several months later.

During our time there, God opened a door for us to meet with the mayor of one of the districts of Lima. When we arrived for our appointment, the mayor's assistant met with us, explaining that the mayor was called away to an important meeting.

While visiting with the official, I took the opportunity to share Jesus with him. He told me that his wife was a follower of Jesus, but he was not. I shared the Good News with him and asked if he wanted to give his life to Jesus! He looked at me and smiled and said, "Yes! I want to give my life to Jesus!"

It was so exciting to lead this dear man to faith in Jesus Christ right in the Mayor's office! All for Jesus!

God has given me a boldness to approach people in conversation about the Lord. Perhaps you have the same style as me, or maybe God has given you something different. The main thing is that no matter how God has wired you, He wants you to get in the game and live a life actively sharing Jesus with your friends!

FIVE STYLES

Pastor Bill Hybels and Mark Mittelberg wrote a book called *Becoming a Contagious Christian*. The authors describe five different evangelistic styles in the book. You may be strong in one of more of these styles. The bottom line is that, hopefully, you will be encouraged to know that you can share Jesus in ways that fit how God has designed you.

1. CONFRONTATIONAL STYLE

The confrontational style is all about being bold and direct in sharing the Good News of Jesus. The way I shared the Gospel with the mayor's assistant and the way I share on stage fits this style.

Two more contemporary examples are Billy Graham and Luis Palau when they publically address crowds. Very few people I have talked with identify confrontational as there their strongest style.

For a biblical example of confrontational style, we can look at Peter in Acts 2 at Pentecost. Acts 2:40 says about Peter's message, "with many other words he warned them; and he pleaded with them."

2. INVITATIONAL STYLE

This style is all about friends bringing friends to Jesus, like Andrew did with his brother Peter (see John 1:41-42). The invitational style is simply inviting your friend to "Come and See" who Jesus is by inviting them to a Christian Church, festival, or event.

A recent survey revealed that the majority of unbelievers said they would go to church or a Christian event if a friend invited them. Who is in your life right now that the Lord is leading you to invite to church or an event?

I love how Philip invited his friend Nathanael to meet Jesus in John 1:45-46. "Philip found Nathanael and told him, 'We have found the one Moses wrote about in the Law, and about whom the prophets also wrote – Jesus of Nazareth, the son of Joseph.'

'Nazareth! Can anything good come from there?' Nathanael asked.

'Come and see,' said Philip."

When you invite people to hear about Jesus, you are using the invitation style to reach people for Jesus!

A few years ago we were holding a festival in Sri Lanka. A woman came to the festival and gave her life to Jesus! She went home and invited her sister to the festival. Her sister came, heard about Jesus for herself, and gave her life to Him! Isn't that awesome?

3. INTELLECTUAL STYLE

The third evangelistic style uses apologetics to "defend" the faith in sharing the Gospel. People with the intellectual style use historical facts and God's Word to share the Good News of Jesus with people that want answers. A great example of this is the Apostle Paul when he shared the Good News of Jesus on Mars Hill (see Acts 17:16-34).

If you think the Intellectual Style is your greatest strength I encourage you to read two books from author Lee Strobel called *The Case for Christ* and *The Case for Faith*. These two books will sharpen you as you use the Intellectual Style to bring your friends to Jesus!

4. TESTIMONIAL STYLE

The majority of people I've talked with about evangelistic styles find this one to be the most natural. This style uses your personal testimony to share Jesus with others.

In John 4:28-29, we read about the woman at the well: "Then, leaving her water jar, the woman went back to the town and said to the people, 'Come, see a man who told me everything I ever did. Could this be the Christ?'"

I love how this woman used her testimony of meeting Jesus and how God used it to reach the people in her town. Later in that same chapter, we learn the woman's testimony (John 4:39-42):

> *"Many of the Samaritans from that town believed in Him because of the woman's testimony, 'He told me everything I ever did.' So when the Samaritans came to Him, they urged Him to stay with them, and He stayed two days. And because of His words many more became believers.*
>
> *They said to the woman, 'We no longer believe just because of what you said; now we have heard for ourselves, and we know that this man really is the Savior of the world."*

The people first believed because of the woman's testimony; but then they also met and heard Jesus themselves, so their faith became more solidified. May it be so for you and me – that people will believe because of our story, but then enter into their own relationship with Jesus.

5. SERVICE STYLE

Service style demonstrates the love of Jesus through action. Dorcas was described in Acts 9:36 as "always doing good and helping the poor." Showing the love of Jesus through serving others often opens a door to sharing Jesus with our words.

Many of the mission teams over the years have included men and women who work in the medical field. Our medical team has gone to remote places of the earth where few have even heard the name of Jesus. One of these places was Nepal.

While I was at the medical clinic in Nepal, I asked our medical team leader and good friend, Brandon Schmidgall, to come out of the clinic and share his testimony with all the patients waiting to be seen. After Brandon finished sharing his testimony, I told the crowd about the Great Physician, Jesus Christ, who came to meet their spiritual needs on the Cross. At that medical clinic many people who were served gave their lives to Jesus!

You may or may not be gifted medically, but there are ways that God has equipped you to serve others. Selfishness and pride are rampant – it's part of our nature apart from Christ. But if we live as Jesus did, we humble ourselves and put others before us.

It's amazing how caring for someone else's needs often causes them to be receptive to, and sometimes even initiate a conversation about, the reason for your hope.

Acts of service could be anything that meets the needs of others: raking leaves for a neighbor who is too weak to do it himself, taking notes for a classmate who is sick, buying groceries for a friend who lost a job, visiting a relative in the hospital, taking care of someone's pet when they're out of town, or helping a new student find their way around school. The list could go on and on. I hope this sparks some ideas of your own.

TAKE THE EVANGELISTIC STYLE CHALLENGE

Go back and prayerfully select one, two, or even three of the evangelistic styles you think are your best fit. Then write in the margin next to the style(s) the names of friends you have that you think would respond best to that style.

Pray and ask God for open doors to use that style with your friend. Finally, set up a plan to meet with your friend and share Jesus with them. You can do this as you rely on the Holy Spirit to work in and through you!

Let's pray.

> *Lord, please help me to understand how you have made me and what style is my sweet spot. Please give me boldness and confidence to share You with others using this style.*
>
> *Abba, I pray for the people you are bringing to mind. Please draw them to Jesus and give me an open door to share Your Good News with them. In Jesus' Name, Amen.*

PULLING IT ALL TOGETHER

You've made it to chapter 15, and it seems like we've come a long way together, doesn't it? As you have read through this book and prayed with me at the end of each chapter, I wonder if your heart and life are beginning to change.

Are you thinking differently about the world around you than when you first picked up this book? Are your relationships more intentional? Are you spending more time praying and memorizing Scripture?

ENDURANCE RUNNING

If you think of the Christian life as a race, we're in a marathon rather than a sprint. To be a runner, it takes self-discipline, mental toughness, and physical conditioning. Our spiritual race has many parallels. God wants us to know that there is a prize, so we need to focus on finishing.

At times, it is tempting to look back at what God has done and think, "Maybe I've done enough." But the Apostle Paul, even though he had led countless people to Christ, had a different attitude. We get a glimpse of it in Philippians 3:12-14 (*NLT*):

I don't mean to say that I have already achieved these things or that I have already reached perfection. But I press on to possess that perfection for which Christ Jesus first possessed me. No, dear brothers and sisters, I have not achieved it, but I focus on this one thing: Forgetting the past and looking forward to what lies ahead, I press on to reach the end of the race and receive the heavenly prize for which God, through Christ Jesus, is calling us.

Paul never settled for what he accomplished in the past. He kept pressing on for what was ahead. Don't get me wrong, it's good for us to celebrate the victories. But let's not get stuck there. We want to keep growing, reaching more people, and making disciples as long as we live.

The author of Hebrews reminds us that we're being watched. Imagine you're in an Olympic arena, and everyone in the stands are men, women, and kids who have lived and died in faith. Knowing that they're cheering us on, we're encourage to run with nothing holding us back, and to run with endurance (*NLT*, Hebrews 12:1-4):

Therefore, since we are surrounded by such a huge crowd of witnesses to the life of faith, let us strip off every weight that slows us down, especially the sin that so easily trips us up. And let us run with endurance the race God has set before us. We do this by keeping our eyes on Jesus, the champion who initiates and perfects our faith. Because of the joy awaiting him, he endured the cross, disregarding its shame. Now he is seated in the place of honor beside God's throne. Think of all the hostility he endured from sinful people; then you won't become weary and give up. After all, you have not yet given your lives in your struggle against sin.

I can't wait to see what's ahead for you and me as we read and obey these words in Scripture. Let's do it! Let's run with endurance this race God has for us! Let's pray faithfully and get into God's Word like we can't live without it. Let's love people like Jesus does and teach them about Him by our example and our words.

ETHIOPIA – NEVER GIVE UP!

In 2013, our team held a festival in a desperately unreached city on the border of war-torn Sudan. In fact, it was the first open-air, public proclamation of the Gospel in more than 20 years! This part of Ethiopia was extremely dangerous and there was strong opposition to the Gospel there. The churches united to reach their city for Jesus. They had been praying for a great harvest.

On the first night of our festival, people packed into the site. I could hear children playing on the field as cars drove by on the road parallel to the festival grounds. A warm, gentle breeze rustled the branches of a tree near the stage.

Standing near the stage while musicians played, I prayed and prepared to share Jesus with the crowd. As I got up to preach, I sensed the Holy Spirit preparing my heart for the battle ahead. As I preached the Good News of Jesus, I felt a huge weight on my chest. I have felt spiritual battles many times while preaching the Gospel, but never before like this. It felt as if I was running uphill as I preached. I was exhausted spiritually and physically.

The moment came for me to give the invitation for people to receive Jesus. I could never have imagined what happened next!

As I called people to raise their hands if they wanted to receive Jesus, about 200 men stormed right in front of the stage, screaming and shouting in protest that I had just preached Jesus!

These men were from another religion and they were not happy about my message. I stood there in shock, wondering if this was it. Was I going to become a martyr for Jesus in Ethiopia? We had security at the festival, but they fled in fear of losing their own lives.

I pictured my dear wife Carmen and my three kids, Azlan, Mylie, and Tobin, in my mind as the men rushed toward me. I prayed fervently that God would intervene and save my life and the lives of the people that just gave their lives to Him. I prayed that God would move in the hearts of those men who were yelling and shaking their fists.

The mob of angry men passed in front of me and started banging on the wall outside the festival grounds.

Praise be to God! The mob had left!

I was thankful to still be alive, but I was also shaken and discouraged. I stood on the stage wondering, "Why would these men do such a thing?" I knew why, but during tough times it can be hard to see through the fog of confusion.

As I stood there discouraged about the altar call being disturbed by the protest, a young Ethiopian boy, probably the age of my son Azlan, came up to me and handed me a note that said, "Never give up!"

While Jesus promised to be with us, He never said it would be easy to be a witness for Him. No matter what, keep sharing Jesus with others! And never give up!

I hope you found some inspiration and encouragement in *Active8*. I'm praying that it is a resource you will use again and again. And please, share this book with others who can use it too. It's full of tools from God's Word and people around the world who have been actively sharing their faith with others.

Please write to me at stories@reidsaunders.org or post a comment on Facebook.com/ReidSaundersAssociation to let me know what you found helpful, if you have a story of sharing the Good News, and/or to let me know you'd like to get a copy of this for someone else. It would be a great blessing to me and my team to hear how the Lord is using this book to encourage His people.

Hold onto the promise that Jesus made in Matthew 28:20, "And be sure of this: I am with you always, even to the end of the age." Jesus wants you to make disciples; but He doesn't send you into the world alone, He is the one walking with you! He is the one who is seeking through you. He is the one loving and speaking through you.

Let's pray together, one last time in this book.

Abba, thank you for these dear brothers and sisters who have trekked on this Active8 journey with me. Please bless them for their willingness to read, pray, and memorize your Word. Thank you for being with them, and giving each of us the assurance that You will always be with us.

Please pour out Your Spirit and Your favor on each of us as we walk in this ministry of reconciliation that you have entrusted to us. Please help us to put on the full armor of God from Ephesians 6 and stand firm, taking our stand against the evil one who seeks to steal, kill, and destroy.

Thank You for your patience and desire for all to come to repentance. Please help us to see people like You do, to love them like Jesus loves us, and to serve them as Your Holy Spirit empowers us.

Thank You for choosing us before the creation of the world to be holy and blameless, for adopting us into sonship through the blood of Your Son, and for preparing good works in advance for us to do. Now help us to faithfully walk in those good works. Please grant us a harvest of souls as we labor in Your ripe fields. In Jesus' Name, Amen.

RESOURCES AND
QUICK REFERENCE

PRAYER OF DECISION

Think of it! Right now you can become a child of God and a part of His family! You can begin a personal relationship with Jesus Christ by praying to God. This prayer doesn't save you; your faith in Jesus does, but it simply confirms the decision you have just made in your heart. Pray this right now.

> *Dear God, I know that I am have sinned. I have done and said things that have hurt You and others. I turn to You in faith, believing that You sent Your Son, Jesus Christ, to pay the debt for my sins when He died on the cross. I believe that three days later Jesus rose from the dead. Come into my heart, Lord Jesus. Forgive me of my sins. I receive your free gift of eternal life through faith in Jesus right now. In His Name I pray, Amen.*

THE FULL ARMOR OF GOD

I should warn you. If you really want to make disciples, prepare for battle. The enemy of our souls is on the prowl:

> *Stay alert! Watch out for your great enemy, the devil. He prowls around like a roaring lion, looking for someone to devour. Stand firm against him, and be strong in your faith. Remember that your family of believers all over the world is going through the same kind of suffering you are* (*NLT*, 1 Peter 5:8-9).

Jesus warned us, too: "The thief's purpose is to steal and kill and destroy. My purpose is to give them a rich and satisfying life" (*NLT*, John 10:10).

We don't ever want to run or turn our backs on the enemy. Our job is to stand firm and resist. He's the one who will do the running! James tells us, "So humble yourselves before God. Resist the devil, and he will flee from you" (*NLT*, James 4:7).

The best way for us to resist Satan's attacks is by putting on the full armor of God, as described in Ephesians 6:10-20 (*NLT*):

A final word: Be strong in the Lord and in his mighty power. Put on all of God's armor so that you will be able to stand firm against all strategies of the devil. For we are not fighting against flesh-and-blood enemies, but against evil rulers and authorities of the unseen world, against mighty powers in this dark world, and against evil spirits in the heavenly places.

Therefore, put on every piece of God's armor so you will be able to resist the enemy in the time of evil. Then after the battle you will still be standing firm. Stand your ground, putting on the belt of truth and the body armor of God's righteousness. For shoes, put on the peace that comes from the Good News so that you will be fully prepared. In addition to all of these, hold up the shield of faith to stop the fiery arrows of the devil. Put on salvation as your helmet, and take the sword of the Spirit, which is the word of God.

Pray in the Spirit at all times and on every occasion. Stay alert and be persistent in your prayers for all believers everywhere.

And pray for me, too. Ask God to give me the right words so I can boldly explain God's mysterious plan that the Good News is for Jews and Gentiles alike. I am in chains now, still preaching this message as God's ambassador. So pray that I will keep on speaking boldly for him, as I should.

I hope you'll spend time studying the armor of God and meditate on it, even memorize it. Spiritual attack comes our way as we seek God earnestly and actively share our faith. So, when you are attacked, take courage. The enemy wouldn't target you if you weren't a threat!

IMPORTANT BIBLE REFERENCES (IN BIBLICAL ORDER)

Isaiah 59:2, "But your iniquities have separated you from your God; your sins have hidden his face from you, so that He will not hear."

Zechariah 4:6, "This is the word of the Lord to Zerubbabel: 'Not by might nor by power, but by my Spirit,' says the Lord Almighty."

Matthew 28:16-20 (*NLT*), "Jesus came and told his disciples, "I have been given all authority in heaven and on earth. Therefore, go and make disciples of all the nations, baptizing them in the name of the Father and the Son and the Holy Spirit. Teach these new disciples to obey all the commands I have given you. And be sure of this: I am with you always, even to the end of the age."

Luke 19:10, "For the Son of Man came to seek and save those who are lost."

John 1:12, "Yet to all who received Him, to those who believed in his Name, he gave the right to become children of God...."

John 3:16, "For God so loved the world that he gave his one and only Son, that whoever believes in him shall not perish but have eternal life."

John 10:10, "...I have come that they may have life, and have it to the full."

John 14:6, "I am the way and the truth and the life. No one comes to the Father except through me."

John 16:7-11, "But I tell you the truth: It is for your good that I am going away. Unless I go away, the Counselor will not come to you; but if I go, I will send Him to you. When He comes, He will convict the world of guilt in regard to sin and righteousness and judgment: in regard to sin, because men do not believe in Me; in regard to righteousness, because I am going to the Father, where you can see me no longer; and in regard to judgment, because the prince of this world now stands condemned."

Acts 3:19, "Repent, then, and turn to God, so that your sins may be wiped out, that times of refreshing may come from the Lord."

Acts 4:12, "Salvation is found in no one else, for there is no other name under heaven given to men by which we must be saved."

Romans 3:10-12, "There is no one righteous, not even one; there is no one who understands, no one who seeks God. All have turned away, they have together become worthless; there is no one who does good, not even one."

Romans 10:17, "Faith comes from hearing the message, and the message is heard through the word of Christ."

1 Corinthians 15:3-6, "I passed on to you what was most important and what had also been passed on to me. Christ died for our sins, just as the Scriptures said. He was buried, and he was raised from the dead on the third day, just as the Scriptures said. He was seen by Peter and then by the Twelve. After that, he was seen by more than 500 of his followers at one time."

2 Corinthians 4:7 (*NLT*), "We now have this light shining in our hearts, but we ourselves are like fragile clay jars containing this great treasure. This makes it clear that our great power is from God, not from ourselves."

2 Corinthians 5:14-15, "For Christ's love compels us, because we are convinced that one died for all, and therefore all died. And he died for all, that those who live should no longer live for themselves but for him who died for them and was raised again."

2 Corinthians 5:21 (*NLT*), "For God made Christ, who never sinned, to be the offering for our sin, so that we could be made right with God through Christ."

2 Corinthians 6:1-2, "As God's partners, we beg you not to accept this marvelous gift of God's kindness and then ignore it. For God says, 'At just the right time, I heard you. On the day of salvation, I helped you.' Indeed, the 'right time' is now. Today is the day of salvation."

Ephesians 2:8-9, "For it is by grace you have been saved, through faith – and this not from yourselves, it is the gift of God – not by works, so that no one can boast."

2 Thessalonians 1:8-9, "He will punish those who do not know God and do not obey the gospel of our Lord Jesus. They will be punished with everlasting destruction and shut out from the presence of the Lord and from the majesty of his power...."

Philemon 1:6, "I pray that you may be active in sharing your faith, so that you will have a full understanding of every good thing we have in Christ."

James 5:16, "The prayer of a righteous person is powerful and effective."

1 Peter 3:12, "For the eyes of the Lord are on the righteous and His ears are attentive to their prayers."

1 Peter 3:15, "But in your hearts set apart Christ as Lord. Always be prepared to give an answer to everyone who asks you to give the reason for the hope that you have. But do this with gentleness and respect."

2 Peter 3:9 (*NLT*), "The Lord isn't really being slow about his promise, as some people think. No, he is being patient for your sake. He does not want anyone to be destroyed, but wants everyone to repent."

1 John 1:9 (*NLT*), "But if we confess our sins to him, he is faithful and just to forgive us our sins and to cleanse us from all wickedness."

WEB AND MOBILE RESOURCES

https://www.biblegateway.com/
Bible Gateway is a free online tool where you can access many different Bible versions in English and other languages. Bible Gateway also has apps for your mobile devices. You can

access several types of reading plans, study materials, and newsletters. A few audio Bible versions are also available to listen to (stream) for free.

https://dailyaudiobible.com/
Daily Audio Bible is a free online resource for listening to the Bible. Each day, Brian Hardin reads from four sections of Scripture, in the following order: an Old Testament book, a New Testament Book, Psalms, and Proverbs. January 1 begins with Genesis 1, Matthew 1, Psalm 1, and Proverbs 1. During the course of the year, if you listen every day, you'll hear the entire Bible by December 31. The daily podcast also includes Brian's commentary/teaching and community prayers and requests from callers around the globe. An app for mobile devices is available for a minimal fee.

http://nextgenerationalliance.org/
Founded by Luis Palau Association, Next Generation Alliance serves to equip evangelists around the world with encouragement, ideas, networking, and tools to reach people with the Good News. Their website helps people connect with evangelists and their events. It's also a great place to get ideas and see how God is working in the world.

https://www.cru.org/
Cru, formerly known as Campus Crusade for Christ, has many free resources for sharing your faith. On their "How to Know God" page, you'll find links for sharing your faith with many different groups of people, including intellectuals, people from other religions, and more.

http://crustore.org/fourlawseng.htm
Cru developed the "Four Spiritual Laws," along with illustrations. The four laws have been used by millions of people for decades as a simple, easy-to-remember way to share the Gospel with others. You can view the four laws at this website, and order small booklets of it if you wish.

http://soulthirstdisciplemaking.com/
http://www.reallifeministries.com/discipleshift1/
http://www.sonlife.com/training-events/
In disciple making training offered by Soul Thirst, Real Life Ministries, or Sonlife, you'll look in-depth at how Jesus made disciples in the Gospels and the implications that has for you and me in the twenty-first century.

http://www.dare2share.org
Dare 2 Share's website is a great resource for sharing the Gospel, especially with teenagers. There are countless links, including videos, books, help with understanding various worldviews, and seeker websites that you can share with others.

http://www.lifein6words.com/
The Lifein6Words.com seeker Website features the popular YouTube video, Life in 6 Words: The GOSPEL. The site walks seekers through the message of the gospel, invites them to connect with God, encourages them to search out answers if they have more questions, and provides those who put their trust in Jesus with helpful next steps on their new journey.

Dare 2 Share Mobile App
The engaging Dare 2 Share app motivates and equips Christians to share their faith by putting free faith-sharing training and tools directly into their hands. It focuses on a relational sharing approach that encourages give-and-take dialogue, while coaching users through the basics of sharing a clear gospel message. Available from iTunes, Google Play, and Windows Phone.

Life in 6 Words Mobile App
With the interactive Life in 6 Words mobile app, you can use your phone to start spiritual conversations. The striking graphics help you clearly communicate Jesus' invitation to trust in Him, both visually and verbally. Available from iTunes and Google Play.

Gospel Advancing Ministry App
This app trains youth/church leaders how to build a Gospel Advancing Ministry. Available from iTunes and Google Play.

Life in 6 Words

Sharing the gospel with someone is like taking them on a journey through the story of the Bible. This journey can be explained in a six-letter acrostic that spells out the word GOSPEL (© Dare 2 Share Ministries 2016, used by permission).

GOD created us to be with Him.

OUR sins separate us from God.

SINS cannot be removed by good deeds.

PAYING the price for sin, Jesus died and rose again.

EVERYONE who trusts in Him alone has eternal life.

LIFE with Jesus starts now and lasts forever.

WORKS CITED

- Billy Graham Evangelistic Association. *The Mission of an Evangelist: A Conference of Preaching Evangelists*. Minneapolis: World Wide Publications, 2001. Print.
- Hybels, Bill and Mark Mittelberg. *Becoming a Contagious Christian*. Grand Rapids: Zondervan, 1994. Print.
- Reid Saunders Association. *Stories from the Ends of the Earth*. Charleston: CreateSpace Independent Publishing Platform, 2013. Print.
- Swindoll, Charles R. *Swindoll's Ultimate Book of Illustrations & Quotes*. Nashville: Thomas Nelson, 1998. Print.

OTHER BOOKS FROM REID SAUNDERS ASSOCIATION

- *All for Jesus! Making Your Life Count for Christ*
- *Life to the Fullest: Discover the Joy of Living All for Jesus*
- *Stories from the Ends of the Earth*

RECOMMENDED READING

- *The Case for Christ* by Lee Strobel
- *The Case for Faith* by Lee Strobel
- *Complete Evangelism Guidebook* by Scott Dawson
- *Dare 2 Share: A Field Guide to Sharing your Faith* by Greg Stier
- *Gospelize your Youth Ministry* by Greg Stier
- *Just As I Am* by Billy Graham
- *Just Walk Across the Room* by Bill Hybels
- *The Next Christians: Seven Ways You Can Live the Gospel and Restore the World* by Gabe Lyons
- *No Compromise: The Life Story of Keith Green* by Melody Green
- *A Passion for Souls: The Life of DL Moody* by Lyle W. Dorsett

ABOUT REID SAUNDERS

Reid was born and raised in Petaluma, California. At seventeen years of age, Reid surrendered himself to the Lord, a decision that changed the trajectory of his life. As a young Christ-follower, Reid recorded many of Billy Graham's messages, marveling at the power of God's Word to touch hearts and change lives.

He attended Corban University in Salem, Oregon and Multnomah Biblical Seminary in Portland, Oregon, where Reid received his Master of Divinity. He also gained valuable training and experience as in intern at Luis Palau Association.

Reid Saunders Association (RSA) was founded in 2002. Since then, RSA has proclaimed the Gospel in word and deed to more than sixty-nine million people through their global ministry, including face-to-face presentations with more than two million people in sixty-nine countries.

Reid and his wife Carmen have been married for 17 years and have three children: Azlan, Mylie, and Tobin. The Saunders family lives in Salem, Oregon. Together, the family has gone on a mission trip to Oaxaca, Mexico.

During the summers, Reid often takes one or more of the kids along for a festival or speaking engagement. It's exciting to see Azlan, Mylie, and Tobin following in their parents' footsteps and growing in their desire to serve others and share the Good News of Jesus Christ.

ABOUT SHANNON BUTCHER

Shannon was born and raised in Tacoma, Washington, and accepted Christ at the age of fifteen at church camp. She began growing in the Lord through youth group and Bible studies, and went on two mission trips with her youth group to Ensenada, Mexico.

She graduated from Multnomah University with a Bachelor of Science in Biblical Studies and Music Ministry. During college, she served on mission trips to Dominican Republic and Croatia, and met her husband Brett. Shannon and Brett began serving with Reid Saunders Association as volunteers in 2004 and joined the staff the next year.

Together, Brett and Shannon have traveled around the world with RSA, sharing the Good News of Jesus. They have three children and live in Salem, Oregon.

Currently, Shannon works as a substitute teacher and freelance writer/editor. She founded and leads a sexual abuse prevention ministry (www.innocencefound.org), leads worship, and writes and records songs. She is currently working on releasing a new song, titled "Royalty," in both English and Spanish ("Realeza"). Visit facebook.com/ShannonMButcher/ to follow her music journey.

REID SAUNDERS ASSOCIATION BELIEVES…

The Bible is the infallible Word of God, without error in the original writings, and it has supreme and final authority. RSA believes in One God, eternally existing in three persons – Father, Son and Holy Spirit; in the deity of our Lord Jesus Christ; and that He was conceived by the Holy Spirit, born of the virgin Mary, lived a sinless life, and performed miracles. We believe that Christ died to atone humanity's sins through His shed blood and that He was bodily resurrected.

RSA believes that Jesus ascended and is seated at the right hand of the Father as our mediator and advocate; that one day He will return to earth in power and glory; and that all men everywhere are lost and will face God's judgment and need to come to a saving knowledge of His Son Jesus Christ through His shed blood on the cross.

We believe in the spiritual unity of the Church, which is the Body of Christ composed of all who come to salvation by faith in the Lord Jesus Christ; in holy Christian living, and that we must have compassion for the hurts and social needs of our fellowmen; and in using available modern means of media to spread the Good News of our Lord Jesus Christ through all the world.

RSA SHORT–TERM MISSION TRIPS

RSA short-term mission teams help to spread the Good News in the United States and around the world. People with many different talents and personalities have thrived on RSA trips. Our team members have been involved in medical clinics, clothing distribution, children's ministry, sports outreach, freestyle BMX, skateboarding, music, dance, drama, language interpreting, dental hygiene, vision assessments, prayer teams, health seminars, leadership training, videography, photography, prison outreach, street outreach, school visits, and more.

Every team member has opportunities to share their faith and interact with local people. Most team members also participate in an evangelistic festival or cooperative event. Please consider joining us.

To find a current list of trips, visit the Reid Saunders Association website, www.reidsaunders.org.

Here is what some of our mission team members have shared about their experience with RSA:

Within weeks of meeting Reid, I was signed up to go on my first mission trip to Uganda. The trip was eye-opening and life-changing for me. After my second trip to Uganda, I knew I had to be a part of restoring God's kingdom on earth. My career path took a drastic turn at that point.

Today, I mobilize people from across the United States to serve orphans around the world. The experiences I had with RSA were really pivotal in guiding my life in that direction. I do what I do today because of the passion that I saw in Reid and others in the organization – in the way they wanted to serve and glorify God.

ERICA STILLAR

Orphan Care and Missions Manager at All God's Children International, RSA Mission Team Member (Uganda 2005 and 2007)

I was sitting in church in 2009 when I saw a video about an upcoming RSA mission trip to Sudan. I had never been on a mission trip outside the United States before, but felt compelled to go on this one! That mission trip really changed a lot for me. The travel was incredibly hard and there were a lot of challenges. But it all worked out and was very successful. It was an amazing experience for me and totally changed my heart for missions.

I never really shared my testimony in front of large crowds, but in Sudan I was able to share my story and the Good News of Jesus. Never before had I gone to four schools a day, served in medical clinics, ministered in an orphanage, played Jesus in a drama, and visited a prison. I even got to teach the prisoners how to play ultimate Frisbee. One man in leg shackles managed to run up and down the field.

That trip absolutely changed my life. I've always felt like serving was a spiritual gift of mine. I've always been community service oriented. That trip showed me what serving God was about, and the reason why I serve. I'd go on mission trips all the time if I could afford it. But ultimately, it's not about only trips, missions is about a lifestyle. We are constantly on a mission, no matter where we're placed and what we're doing. But there's something about the command to go out to the ends of the earth that has really touched me in this season of life.

Since going to Sudan in 2009, I've gone to Haiti twice with a different ministry and can't wait to go again. I'm not a doctor, I'm not a pastor. I don't have that to offer. I'm in construction and I do project management for a living. So I go in and build houses and use that to be a witness to these people. My trip to Sudan in 2009 is really what put me on this track of having a heart for international missions – for going out and earning the right and opportunity to share the gospel with people by serving.

CRAIG SHUMATE

RSA Mission Team Member (Sudan 2009)

CONTACT INFORMATION

www.active8me.org

Visit our Active8 website to find some of the tools in this book and more great stuff you'll want to share with your friends.

www.reidsaunders.org

Visit the RSA home page to learn about upcoming events and mission trips, watch videos of Reid and some of our past events, and find out how you can connect with us to reach even more people for Christ.

stories@reidsaunders.org

Please write to us and tell us your story. We'd love to hear from you!

info@reidsaunders.org

Find us on: Facebook – Twitter – YouTube

PO Box 4275
Salem, OR 97306

503-581-7394

TESTIMONY WORKSHEET

On a separate piece of paper or on your computer or phone, write out your answers to the following questions.

BC = Before I accepted Christ

- What problems or feelings did you struggle with?
- What did your life revolve around?
- How did these things let you down?

CC = Commitment to Christ

- When was the first time I heard the Gospel?
- What were my initial reactions?
- When did my attitude begin to change? Why?

WC = Walking with Christ

- What are the specific changes Christ has made in your life?
- What has your life been like since becoming a Christian? Think through the benefits of knowing Christ.

Helpful hints:

Try to write the way you speak – make the testimony yours. Don't exaggerate or be overly dramatic – be truthful and genuine. Practice it over and over again until it becomes natural. Try to keep your testimony between three and five minutes when you say it.

ACTIVE8 VERSE CARDS

Either cut the following cards out or make your own to use for memorizing Active8. Check www.active8me.org for printable resources.

Romans 3:23
"For all have sinned and fall short of the glory of God."

Romans 5:1
"Therefore since we have been justified by faith we have peace with God through our Lord Jesus Christ."

Romans 5:8
"But God demonstrates His own love for us in this: While we were still sinners Christ died for us."

Romans 6:23
"For the wages of sin is death, but the gift of God is eternal life through Christ Jesus our Lord."

Romans 8:1
"Therefore, there is now no condemnation for those who are in Christ Jesus."

Romans 10:9
"If you confess with your mouth, 'Jesus is Lord,' and believe in your heart that God raised him from the dead, you will be saved."

Romans 10:10
"For it is with your heart that you believe and are justified, and it is with your mouth that you confess and are saved."

Romans 10:13
"Everyone who calls on the name of the Lord will be saved."

GOOD NEWS LIST

Either cut the following card out or make your own to use as a reminder to pray for up to five people you know. Check www. active8me.org for printable resources.

List three to five people in your life who don't know Jesus yet. Pray for them daily for the next three months. Pray that God would work on their hearts and draw them to Jesus.

1. _____

2. _____

3. _____

4. _____

5. _____

REID SAUNDERS
ASSOCIATION

Hi Friend,

Here are some great ways that you can follow me as I take the message of the cross to the ends of the earth.

All for Jesus!

CONNECT WITH REID

REIDSAUNDERS.ORG ACTIVE8ME.ORG

FACEBOOK.COM/REIDSAUNDERSASSOCIATION

TWITTER.COM/REIDSAUNDERS

YOUTUBE.COM/REIDSAUNDERSVIDEOS